# The Preeminence & All-Sufficiency of Jesus Christ

A Brief Exposition of Colossians

Malcolm Webber

Published by:

**Strategic Press**
www.StrategicPress.org

Strategic Press is a division of Strategic Global Assistance, Inc.
www.sgai.org

513 S. Main St. Suite 2
Elkhart, IN 46516
U.S.A

+1-844-532-3371 (LEADER-1)

Copyright © 2000 Malcolm Webber

ISBN 978-1-888810-60-8

All Scripture references are from the New International Version of the Bible, unless otherwise noted.

Printed in the United States of America

## THE CONVENTIONS USED IN THIS BOOK:

## TYPOGRAPHY:

> **THIS FORM (SMALL CAPS AND BOLD) IS USED FOR SECTION HEADINGS.**
>
> ***This form (italics and bold) is used for direct quotes from Colossians.***
>
> When commentary is made on a specific word or phrase, a hanging indent is also used.
>
> Broader commentary is made flush with the left margin.

## CITATIONS:

> When verses from Colossians are cited in the text, the book name is not specified (e.g., 2:9-10).
>
> Cited Scriptures of particular interest are quoted in the footnotes.

# The Purpose of This Exposition

"The Levites…instructed the people in the Law while the people were standing there. They read from the Book of the Law of God, making it clear and giving the meaning so that the people could understand what was being read." (Neh. 8:7-8)

The Levites, under Ezra's oversight, did not take it upon themselves to make exhaustive interpretation and application of every word in the text, but instead simply read the Word of God, "making it clear and giving the meaning so that the people could understand what was being read."

This is the simple purpose of this exposition: to make the Scriptures clear and to give their sense. It is not our purpose to exhaust every possible interpretation or to make lengthy application of the text. We will leave that up to the local leaders into whose care the Holy Spirit has entrusted His flock.

Malcolm Webber, Ph.D.
Strategic Press
Elkhart, Indiana

# The Preeminence and All-Sufficiency of Jesus Christ

## A Brief Exposition of Colossians

Paul wrote this letter to the Colossian believers to combat a complex mixture of heresy that threatened the life of the church. The Colossian heresy blended together some elements of Christianity with Jewish legalism, Greek philosophical speculation and Oriental mysticism. This joining of religions together in exotic hybrids is happening today in both eastern and western countries with the increasing "globalization" of religion. Consequently, Paul's words are of great significance to today's church around the world.

In Colossians, Paul highlights the divine Person and creative and redemptive work of the Lord Jesus Christ. His answer to the false teachings is very simple – the Person of Jesus! The Christian life *is* Jesus Christ. Nothing is higher or more important than Him. There is no other way to the deep things of God.

Jesus is preeminent and all-sufficient. In Him are hidden all the treasures of wisdom and knowledge. Only through the apprehension of Jesus – in experienced union and fellowship with Him – will these treasures ever be revealed. He, truly, is all we need. In Him is the fullness of the Godhead, and we are complete in Him. We need no path to holiness or spiritual maturity other than inward union with Christ.

# COLOSSIANS

# Introduction

## AUTHOR
Colossians is one of Paul's "prison epistles," so called because Paul was in prison when he wrote it (along with Ephesians which is a "twin epistle" to Colossians, Philippians and Philemon). Probably all the prison epistles were written during Paul's Roman imprisonment.

The distant way in which Paul writes that he has "heard" of his audience's faith (1:4) and his description of them as never having seen him face to face (2:1) imply that he neither founded the church in Colosse nor had visited it. Quite likely, Epaphras founded the church (1:6-7). Epaphras is with Paul at the time of this writing (4:12-13). Possibly, Epaphras was a convert of Paul's ministry in Ephesus and had planted the church at Colosse; he is now visiting Paul in prison (cf. Philemon 23) to solicit his advice concerning a dangerous heresy that threatens the Colossian church. Appropriately, Paul assumes a certain authority over the Colossian church even though he has never been there, since he is a "grandfather" of the work through his convert Epaphras and his judgment has now been sought. Paul's purpose is to encourage the saints to remain faithful to the Lord and His Word, and to reject the errors of the false teachers.

## DATE
The letter was probably written early in AD 62.

## RECIPIENTS
The letter was written to the saints at Colosse, a city which was about 100 miles east of Ephesus. Centuries earlier, Colosse had been an economic center in the area, but by Paul's time its influence had waned. Thus, this letter likely addressed a small congregation in an unimpressive town. These Christians are predominantly Gentile (1:21, 27; 2:13).

## THEMES

In this epistle, Paul highlights the divine Person and creative and redemptive work of Christ against devaluation of Christ by a particular heresy that threatens the church at Colosse. Then Paul draws out the practical implications of this high Christology for everyday life and conduct.

The Colossian heresy blends Christianity together with Jewish legalism, Greek philosophic speculation, and Oriental mysticism. Perhaps the location of Colosse on an important trade route linking East and West contributed to the mixed character of the false teaching. This joining of religions together in exotic hybrids is happening today in both Eastern and Western countries with the increasing "globalization" of religion.

All we know of the false teachers is contained in a few brief references to their errors; these references are not systematically given as an analysis of their doctrine, but only as occasion required and for the purpose of confirming the opposite truths. It is likely that the false teachers had at that time no fully developed system (although this did happen later in certain forms of Gnosticism), but only a few prominent tenets, such as those which Paul condemns. They were probably only the exponents of certain prevailing tendencies, rather than the originators of a clearly defined and formal heresy (as contrasted with Acts 15:1[1]).

Moreover, the false teachers' purpose was not to deny Christ, but to dethrone Him with teachings of the angels being the true mediators between God and man, and Christ being one of many "Emanations" of God. Their doctrine did not deny His death but undervalued it, in promoting the pursuit of peace through ceremonial and ascetic practices. Their conscious purpose was not to subvert Christianity but only to perfect it. They were not trying to convert the church to Judaism or to paganism, but to introduce into the church certain mystical views and practices, and certain forms of "super-spiritual" and elite piety. They were promoting alternate and "higher" paths to spiritual maturity.

---

[1] *Some men came down from Judea to Antioch and were teaching the brothers: "Unless you are circumcised, according to the custom taught by Moses, you cannot be saved." (Acts 15:1)*

These teachers were not like the Pharisees or Judaizers with their outward formality, ostentation, judgmentalism, hypocrisy and self-righteousness obtained from obeying the mere letter of the law. They were more like the Essenes: mystics in doctrine, ascetics in practice, endlessly speculating about hidden truth and esoteric spiritual realities.

Paul looked at what was happening in Colosse and, by virtue of his apostolic gifting (cf. 1 Cor. 3:10), recognized these, albeit undeveloped, tendencies and corrected them. His corrections are pertinent to us today.

The general characteristics of the heresy were:
- Detractions from the Person of Jesus Christ. Thus, Paul stresses Jesus' preeminence (1:15-19). In fact, this letter becomes a magnificent presentation of the Person and work of Christ, containing some of the New Testament's most exalted descriptions of Him. Any doctrine or approach that devalues Christ (e.g., Islam, Jehovah's Witnesses or Mormons), or simply does not preeminently stress Him (e.g., "oneness" doctrine, Catholic worship of Mary or going through the saints as intermediaries, the American blending of Christianity with patriotism, the goal of the Christianization of culture, or "putting aside our doctrinal differences" to work together to seek a "higher" goal such as family values, racial reconciliation or social justice for the poor), should be avoided. The Christian life is all about Jesus (2:6-7). Nothing is higher or more important than Him.
- Emphasis on human philosophical speculations divorced from divine revelation (2:8). Thus, Paul stresses the revelation of Jesus Christ in the Word of God (1:28; 2:3). Today's church is tempted with vain speculation regarding postmodernism, etc., all of which has an aura of "deeper knowledge." We must return to the simplicity of the Word of God that reveals the Lord Jesus.
- Elements of Judaism, such as circumcision (2:11; 3:11), rabbinic tradition (2:8), dietary regulations (2:20-22) and Sabbath and festival observances (2:16), which were seen as necessary, not to attain salvation, but to attain a higher level of holiness and spirituality. Thus, Paul stresses that all these things are but the shadows of which the substance is Christ (2:10, 17). Our salvation is gained *and* maintained

only through Him. Modern day: identification with various religious traditions (e.g., Reformed, Baptist, Mennonite, Pentecostal) instead of Christ Himself. We have a different heritage than that of human religions (cf. Matt. 15:3, 9). Regarding festivals and Sabbaths, these are becoming very popular in some circles – not as means of obtaining salvation, but as ways to go "deeper" in God. But we don't go deeper in God by returning to "shadows" that have been abolished. We go deeper in God through increasing knowledge and relationship with the Person of the Lord Jesus Christ as revealed by His Spirit through His Word!

- Preoccupation and fascinated involvement with the angelic realm; the pagan worship of angels as intermediaries keeping the highest God (pure Spirit) unsullied through contact with the (evil) physical universe (2:18). (Orthodox Jews have constructed a hierarchy of angels, but they do not worship them nor do they regard the materiality of the universe as evil.) Thus, Paul stresses the preeminence and all-sufficiency of Christ (2:19). Modern day: preoccupation with angels and demons. For example: casting demons into a box, commanding angels, receiving false angelic revelation (e.g., *Angels on Assignment*) etc. Bible: Angels are our ministers (Heb. 1:14[2]) but we are not to directly command them (they move at God's command), and we are to be preoccupied with Jesus. Moreover, our revelation is to come from the Word of God, which the believer must know (cf. Gal. 1:8[3]).
- Ascetic practices (2:20-23) designed to perfect the believer's holiness. Thus, Paul stresses the reality of the daily Christian life of walking in union with Jesus in His death and resurrection (2:20; 3:1ff). These kinds of practices have always been popular with their appearance of holiness and humility. In reality, however, they are worthless in going deeper in God and usually result in fleshly pride. Moreover, such practices obscure the simplicity of the Christian life. If Satan cannot tempt the believer into sin, he will do the opposite and try to tempt the believer into false holiness with its accompanying spiritual pride!

---

[2] *Are not all angels ministering spirits sent to serve those who will inherit salvation? (Heb. 1:14)*

[3] *But even if we or an angel from heaven should preach a gospel other than the one we preached to you, let him be eternally condemned! (Gal. 1:8)*

- Exclusivistic secrecy and superiority. Thus, Paul stresses the all-inclusiveness and publicity of the gospel (1:5-6, 20, 23, 28; 3:11). Today, many groups around the world live in the delusion that they have some "deeper light" than everyone else, resulting in carnal pride and sectarianism, and sometimes even in secrecy (in an extraordinary contradiction of Mark 16:15). Such characteristics are infallible indications of error and even cultishness. Moreover, the true gospel is outward looking, rather than existing merely to bring the believer into an exclusive and self-absorbed "Christianity" which is centered on the personal blessings derived from one's privatized relationship with God, and in which the church gathers together to meet personal needs rather than to worship and serve God as an inclusive community (3:12-16).

The Colossian heresy was of the same order of seriousness as the Galatian heresy, except that it centered about the Person of Christ, rather than about salvation by works versus salvation by grace. Paul's answer to the heresy lay not in extended argument, but in a positive presentation of the preeminence and all-sufficiency of Jesus Christ.

Paul's theology is always practical. He is more interested in doing theology than in merely knowing it. Thus, the book has two main sections: doctrine (chaps. 1-2) and exhortation (chaps. 3-4). In the doctrinal section, Paul develops his high doctrine of Christology. In the exhortation section, he shows how that union with Christ in His death, resurrection and ascension forms the basis for Christian living. Believers are to adopt God's perspective by regarding themselves as dead in Christ to sin and alive in Him to righteousness.

# The Book

**1:1-2. PAUL'S GREETING.**

*1:1 Paul, an apostle of Christ Jesus by the will of God, and Timothy our brother,*

*Paul.* Paul had never been to Colosse, but would have been known by name to the Colossian Christians.

*an apostle of Christ Jesus.* Sets forth his authority and credentials to give such a message from God to the church. Paul was personally commissioned by Jesus Christ as an apostle. As elsewhere (e.g., Eph. 1:1; 1 Pet. 1:1), Paul uses the word "apostle" as a statement of his office and function; it is not a title (as in "the apostle Paul"). Paul had legitimate influence with the church at Colosse since he was the spiritual "grandfather" of the work. Apostolic authority is limited in scope (2 Cor. 10:13[4]), relational in nature and respects the local leaders (e.g., 1 Cor. 16:3[5]); it is not universal and absolute.

*by the will of God.* Emphasizes his divinely-bestowed authority and his right to share these words. It is not merely the "will of man" behind Paul. He did not personally choose to become an apostle, nor was he given the position by other men. Note the simplicity and humility of Paul's description of his qualifications ("an apostle of Jesus Christ by the will of God"). He does not emphasize his learning, experience or other human qualifications – he does do this in Phil. 3:4-8 (he describes his human achievements as "dung") and 2 Cor. 11 – 12 (he describes such boasting talk as "foolishness"). Nevertheless, as a godly leader, Paul was still genuinely accountable (Acts 13:1-4; 15:36-41; 21:17-26; Gal 2:1-2; 2 Cor. 4:2; 5:11-12) – he was fully dependent on God, yet not independent of man.

---

[4] *We, however, will not boast beyond proper limits, but will confine our boasting to the field God has assigned to us, a field that reaches even to you. (2 Cor. 10:13)*
[5] *Then, when I arrive, I will give letters of introduction to the men you approve and send them with your gift to Jerusalem. (1 Cor. 16:3)*

***and Timothy our brother.*** Timothy, like Paul, was probably known by name to the Colossian saints. The only title that Paul gives Timothy (who had an apostolic ministry) here is "our brother."

**2 To the holy and faithful brothers in Christ at Colosse: Grace and peace to you from God our Father.**

***To the holy and faithful brothers in Christ.*** Greek = "to the saints and faithful brothers in Christ." They are both names for the same group of people. There is no singling out of the "faithful" from among those who are less faithful (cf. Eph. 1:1.[6] All of God's children are "saints" – they have been separated from sin and this world to become God's own special people. Moreover, they are all "faithful" – they are trusting only in Christ, serving only Him.

***at Colosse.*** Greek = "in Colosse." The saints are "in Christ" and "in Colosse." Being assaulted with false teachings, the saints are struggling to connect their lives in Christ with their lives in Colosse. Their religious observance is tending toward moral asceticism, esoteric philosophical speculation and spiritual mysticism, which actually disconnect them from the world around them. In the parallel of "in Christ" and "in Colosse" Paul reconnects the life of faith with the material world.

It was probably a small group of people in this church; yet, Paul was deeply concerned for them and went to a great deal of trouble on their behalf.

### 1:3-12. Paul's Prayer.

A chiasmus (from a Greek word that means "marked with an X") is a literary pattern used by some skillful writers to draw attention to certain points. In a passage formed in a chiastic pattern, the author presents a sequence of key ideas and then repeats the same ideas in inverted order. What distinguishes a chiasmus from an "inverted parallelism," found frequently in the Old Testament psalms, is the presence of a new idea found between the two inverted sequences. This pivotal idea – the chiastic "vertex" – expresses the chief

---

[6] *Paul, an apostle of Christ Jesus by the will of God, To the saints in Ephesus, the faithful in Christ Jesus: (Eph. 1:1)*

concern around which the other ideas find their meaning. Paul's prayer is built around two series of three theological ideas (vv. 3-6 and vv. 9-12) with the vertex in between (vv. 7-8):

> **A** We always thank God, the Father of our Lord Jesus Christ, when we pray for you, (v. 3)
>> **B** because we have heard of your faith in Christ Jesus and of the love you have for all the saints – the faith and love that spring from the hope that is stored up for you in heaven (vv. 4-5a)
>>> **C** and that you have already heard about in the word of truth, the gospel that has come to you. All over the world this gospel is bearing fruit and growing, just as it has been doing among you since the day you heard it and understood God's grace in all its truth. (vv. 5b-6)
>>>> **D** You learned it from Epaphras, our dear fellow servant, who is a faithful minister of Christ on our behalf, and who also told us of your love in the Spirit. (vv. 7-8)
>>> **C'** For this reason, since the day we heard about you, we have not stopped praying for you and asking God to fill you with the knowledge of his will through all spiritual wisdom and understanding. And we pray this in order that you may live a life worthy of the Lord and may please him in every way: bearing fruit in every good work, growing in the knowledge of God, being strengthened with all power according to his glorious might (vv. 9-11a)
>> **B'** so that you may have great endurance and patience, and joyfully (v. 11b)
> **A'** giving thanks to the Father, who has qualified you to share in the inheritance of the saints in the kingdom of light. (v. 12)

First (A/A'), Paul gives thanks to God, because he has heard reports of the Colossians' piety, described by two related triads of good works (B, faith, love and hope, and B', endurance, patience and joy). He concludes by interpreting their piety to be the natural fruit and logical growth of receiving the truth of the gospel (C/C'). In the middle of his prayer, Paul mentions the ministry of faithful Epaphras (D) through whom the gospel was brought to the Colossians. Paul thus makes Epaphras the pivotal focus of the prayer and presents him as an example of the true Christian life that he desires for the Colossian believers.

### 1:3-8. Paul gives thanks for the report he has received from Epaphras regarding the spiritual welfare of the Colossians.

As he often does, Paul begins this letter with an expression of his gratitude to God for the Christian graces of his readers, thus affirming and encouraging them before dealing with the pertinent issues that gave occasion for his letter. Leadership principle: when you have something to correct, first share many good things to affirm those you are correcting.

Verses 3-8 are a single sentence.

*3 We always thank God, the Father of our Lord Jesus Christ, when we pray for you,*

**We.** Both Paul and Timothy.
**always thank God.** Paul's prayers were consistently filled with thanksgiving. Prayer with thanksgiving was not only Paul's command (e.g., Phil. 4:6[7]) but also his practice.
**we pray for you.** Much prayer is being offered for the Colossians (1:9; 2:1; 4:12; cf. Gal. 4:19).

*4 because we have heard of your faith in Christ Jesus and of the love you have for all the saints –*

**because.** The ground of Paul's thanksgiving is the content of the good report he has received.
**your faith in Christ Jesus and of the love you have for all the saints.** Faith toward God and love towards the brethren are the two most distinguishing

---

[7] *Do not be anxious about anything, but in everything, by prayer and petition, with thanksgiving, present your requests to God. (Phil. 4:6)*

marks of the believer (cf. Eph. 1:15[8]; 2 Thess. 1:3[9]; Philemon 5[10]; 1 John 3:23[11]). True spirituality integrates one's vertical relationship with God and one's horizontal relationships and responsibilities toward man.

**all the saints.** Not only those of your own little group (the attitude of "we're the select of the elect" is an infallible mark of error). Paul begins to attack the exclusivity of the heresy.

**5 the faith and love that spring from the hope that is stored up for you in heaven and that you have already heard about in the word of truth, the gospel**

**the faith and love that spring from the hope.** Their faith and love are grounded in, and partially motivated by, their hope of final salvation and reward in eternity. Cf. 2 Cor. 9:6[12]; Gal. 6:9[13]; Matt. 5:12[14]; 6:20[15]; 19:21[16]; Luke 12:34[17]; 1 Pet. 1:4.[18] The hope of eternal reward is not the deepest reason or motivation for the saints' faith and love (a deeper motive may be simple love for God in spite of any rewards), but it is an authentic and

---

[8] *For this reason, ever since I heard about your faith in the Lord Jesus and your love for all the saints, (Eph. 1:15)*

[9] *We ought always to thank God for you, brothers, and rightly so, because your faith is growing more and more, and the love every one of you has for each other is increasing. (2 Thess. 1:3)*

[10] *because I hear about your faith in the Lord Jesus and your love for all the saints. (Philemon 5)*

[11] *And this is his command: to believe in the name of his Son, Jesus Christ, and to love one another as he commanded us. (1 John 3:23)*

[12] *Remember this: Whoever sows sparingly will also reap sparingly, and whoever sows generously will also reap generously. (2 Cor. 9:6)*

[13] *Let us not become weary in doing good, for at the proper time we will reap a harvest if we do not give up. (Gal. 6:9)*

[14] *Rejoice and be glad, because great is your reward in heaven, for in the same way they persecuted the prophets who were before you. (Matt. 5:12)*

[15] *But store up for yourselves treasures in heaven, where moth and rust do not destroy, and where thieves do not break in and steal. (Matt. 6:20)*

[16] *Jesus answered, "If you want to be perfect, go, sell your possessions and give to the poor, and you will have treasure in heaven. Then come, follow me." (Matt. 19:21)*

[17] *For where your treasure is, there your heart will be also. (Luke 12:34)*

[18] *and into an inheritance that can never perish, spoil or fade – kept in heaven for you, (1 Pet. 1:4)*

biblical encouragement of the same. Moreover, God made us to desire eternal reward so it is not wrong to do so (the problem occurs when our motive becomes a desire for temporal reward). It is false and affectatious spirituality that pretends to not want rewards at all. Notice also, Paul's characteristic combination of faith, hope and love (1 Thess. 1:3; 1 Cor. 13:13; Rom. 5:1-5; 12:6-12).

*the hope that is stored up for you in heaven.* Deposited, reserved, stored out of the reach of all enemies. Cf. 1 Pet. 1:4. Your true treasure is stored in heaven. Moreover, this hope is absolutely certain, unlike many human "hopes" that are merely wishes.

*you have already heard about.* When the gospel was preached to you.

*the word of truth, the gospel.* The word that contains the truth. In contrast to the errors of the false teachers.

**6 that has come to you. All over the world this gospel is bearing fruit and growing, just as it has been doing among you since the day you heard it and understood God's grace in all its truth.**

*All over the world.* In contrast to the exclusive nature of the false gospels (cf. v. 23). The observation of many who once were part of little sects but had their eyes opened to the truth is, "I was amazed to learn there are true Christians out there!" The universal nature of the gospel – for all men, from all cultures in all times (Matt. 28:19[19]; Mark 16:15[20]). This is what you are a part of – the great move of God around the world! It is far better to be a little fish in the huge ocean of God's moving than a big fish in an exclusive little backwater.

*this gospel is bearing fruit and growing.* The gospel bears fruit by its own inherent power. Moreover, it does not exhaust itself by bearing fruit (as with, for example, corn); it also grows. The Word of God is alive and powerful (Heb. 4:12). In addition, the truth of the gospel (in contrast to the false gospels) is authenticated by its ever-widening (numerical, quantitative growth) and deepening influence (spiritual growth). These are marks of a healthy work and the true gospel.

---

[19] *Therefore go and make disciples of all nations…* (Matt. 28:19)

[20] *He said to them, "Go into all the world and preach the good news to all creation."* (Mark 16:15)

Healthy churches will grow – all by themselves (cf. Mark 4:28[21]). Therefore, our task is not to try to make our churches grow, but to see that the churches possess healthy characteristics – so that God can add the growth. The church is a living organism. It will grow by itself as long as it remains healthy. Therefore, the church must be protected from errors and heresies that threaten to kill it (Gal. 5:9[22]). The Word of God will bear the fruit as long as it is the word of truth – "truth" is mentioned twice in vv. 5-6. The same principle is true for healthy individual Christian lives and building healthy Christian leaders.

The Word of God brings forth fruit and is the source of true spiritual experiences and "more of God" in your life. Receiving prayer from an anointed servant of God or visiting the latest "revival hot spot" is good for specific needs such as getting saved, receiving deliverance, receiving the baptism in the Holy Spirit or an initial touch from God, or receiving encouragement in times of weariness, etc., but long-term growth and fruitfulness in God is through His Word by His Spirit. There is no substitute for this.

*just as it has been doing among you.* The Colossians know the life-changing power of the true gospel.
*since the day you heard it.* Expresses the further fact that the progress of the gospel has been continuous from the very first.
*you heard it and understood.* You both heard and received (and therefore understood) the gospel.
*understood God's grace.* In contrast with the legalism of the false teachers.
*in all its truth.* You knew the gospel as it truly is, in its genuine reality, in opposition to the errors that have been recently introduced. You knew the truth; stay with it!

**7 You learned it from Epaphras, our dear fellow servant, who is a faithful minister of Christ on our behalf,**

Epaphras was likely the planter of the Colossian church and has remained in connection with the saints ever since (4:12). Here, Paul affirms the word

---

[21] *All by itself the soil (i.e., the seed in the soil) produces grain – first the stalk, then the head, then the full kernel in the head. (Mark 4:28)*
[22] *"A little yeast works through the whole batch of dough." (Gal. 5:9)*

Epaphras spoke and also Epaphras himself. Paul was a healthy leader; he regularly affirmed local churches as well as their leaders. He was not insecure, keeping all the praise for himself.

***You learned it from Epaphras.*** You have learned the truth; stay with it!
***our dear fellow servant.*** Words of humility, equality and affection to Paul's own convert. Paul loved and deeply appreciated those who worked with him in teaching God's Word. There should be no rivalry or competition among God's servants. If we are seeking only to exalt the Lord, then we will appreciate all others who are doing the same.
***a faithful minister of Christ on our behalf.*** Epaphras was a servant of Christ (serving Christ and not himself), and he was also related to Paul's ministry ("on our behalf").

***8 and who also told us of your love in the Spirit.***

You've started on the right road; stay on it!

***your love.*** The chief fruit of the Christian life. You've got the real thing; keep it!
***in the Spirit.*** The Colossians had begun "in the Spirit" – in fellowship with God, allowing the Holy Spirit to direct their lives and express His love through them. You've got the real thing; keep it (Gal. 3:3)[23]!

Paul now proceeds, gently and delicately at first, to touch on matters needing correction.

### 1:9-12. PAUL'S PRAYER FOR THEIR SPIRITUAL MATURITY.

***9 For this reason, since the day we heard about you, we have not stopped praying for you and asking God to fill you with the knowledge of his will through all spiritual wisdom and understanding.***

Paul prays that they would have true knowledge of the will of God, as contrasted with the false teachings.

---

[23] *Are you so foolish? After beginning with the Spirit, are you now trying to attain your goal by human effort? (Gal. 3:3)*

*For this reason.* On account of their faith and love which Epaphras has told Paul about.

*since the day we heard about you.* Cf. v. 4.

*praying for you and asking God.* "Praying" is general; "asking" is specific.

*the knowledge of his will.* God's will regarding your lives as well as His ultimate purposes in Christ (e.g., Eph. 1:9-10[24]).

*spiritual wisdom.* As contrasted with the fleshly wisdom by which the Colossians were in danger of being ensnared (2:8, 18). Spiritual wisdom comes by the inspiration of the Holy Spirit.

**10 And we pray this in order that you may live a life worthy of the Lord and may please him in every way: bearing fruit in every good work, growing in the knowledge of God,**

*in order that you may live a life worthy.* The purpose of the wisdom and understanding of v. 9 is so that you may live a life that is worthy of the Lord, not merely to "know" spiritual truth as an end in itself, divorced from everyday life. True theology will have practical expression, or it is not truth at all. For Paul, doctrine and practice are inseparable. Conversely, if we are to please God we must first know what His will is. There is no blessing for the ignorant! Christian reality is: true knowledge of the Lord Jesus resulting in fruitful lives that please Him.

*live a life worthy of the Lord.* Cf. Eph. 4:1[25]; 1 Thess. 2:12[26]; 3 John 6.[27] You can do this! You can live a life that is worthy of the infinite God! Believers today are no different from the Colossian Christians.

---

[24] *And he made known to us the mystery of his will according to his good pleasure, which he purposed in Christ, to be put into effect when the times will have reached their fulfillment – to bring all things in heaven and on earth together under one head, even Christ. (Eph. 1:9-10)*

[25] *As a prisoner for the Lord, then, I urge you to live a life worthy of the calling you have received. (Eph. 4:1)*

[26] *encouraging, comforting and urging you to live lives worthy of God, who calls you into his kingdom and glory. (1 Thess. 2:12)*

[27] *They have told the church about your love. You will do well to send them on their way in a manner worthy of God. (3 John 6)*

*may please him in every way.* Our purpose and highest motive is to please God in every way, in everything – this pleasing is not to be partial or limited. That is the fruit of true wisdom and understanding. Cf. "men-pleasers" in 3:22.

Then Paul gives four aspects of how the believer's life will be worthy of God and pleasing to Him: bearing fruit, growing in the knowledge of God, being strengthened to endure and giving thanks. These are the characteristics of the life that pleases God, the life that is "worthy" of Him. God tells us how to please Him! God defines what true "success" is, and it is different from much that is called success in the modern church.

*bearing fruit in every good work.* The good works are the fruits of true spirituality. Not merely good talk but good works. Good works are the natural and inevitable result of the new life in God (3:1ff; Eph. 4:7ff).

*growing in the knowledge of God.* Growing maturity in personal knowledge of God (John 17:3[28]).

**11 being strengthened with all power according to his glorious might so that you may have great endurance and patience, and joyfully**

*all power.* Every kind of power: the power to change lives and bear the fruit of the Spirit. This is primarily internal power – to produce character virtues.

*according to.* The power of God strengthens the believer. This strengthening is not from our own natural vitality or energy, but it comes from imparted strength – the power of God within the believer, inward union with Christ.

*his glorious might.* Greek = "the power of His glory." The power to strengthen is an attribute of the glory of God. This is the measure of His strengthening – it is according to the inexhaustible power of His glory! Thus, the believer can rise above anything!

---

[28] *Now this is eternal life: that they may know you, the only true God, and Jesus Christ, whom you have sent. (John 17:3)*

***so that you may have great endurance.*** Endurance is the result of the power of God in your life. This is the tenacity of spirit that still holds on and perseveres in spite of all. The life that demonstrates the power of God's glory is characterized by endurance, patience and joy.

***endurance and patience.*** Not only in sufferings, but generally in the life of the Spirit – through all the trials, temptations and tribulations.

***and joyfully.*** Joyfulness in suffering expresses itself in thankfulness to God (v. 12; 1 Thess. 5:18[29]).

**12 giving thanks to the Father, who has qualified you to share in the inheritance of the saints in the kingdom of light.**

***giving thanks to the Father.*** The final crowning characteristic of the genuine life in God. Joy accompanies our endurance (1 Pet. 1:6-9).

***qualified.*** Greek = "to make capable or fit." Only here and 2 Cor. 3:6 in the New Testament. God made the believers capable through His Spirit by His Son. Refers to our position in Christ. None but the saints can dwell in the light of His kingdom.

***share.*** To participate.

***inheritance.*** Cf. Eph. 1:11[30].

***the kingdom of light.*** Not only in eternity; the children of God are to walk in light on the earth (v. 13; Eph. 5:8[31]; 1 Thess. 5:5[32]; 1 Pet. 2:9[33]; 1 John 1:7[34]; 2:10[35]). Our eternal inheritance is begun here. We participate in this

---

[29] *give thanks in all circumstances, for this is God's will for you in Christ Jesus. (1 Thess. 5:18)*

[30] *In Him also we have obtained an inheritance, being predestined according to the purpose of Him who works all things according to the counsel of His will, (Eph. 1:11, NKJV)*

[31] *For you were once darkness, but now you are light in the Lord. Live as children of light (Eph. 5:8)*

[32] *You are all sons of the light and sons of the day. We do not belong to the night or to the darkness. (1 Thess. 5:5)*

[33] *But you are a chosen people, a royal priesthood, a holy nation, a people belonging to God, that you may declare the praises of him who called you out of darkness into his wonderful light. (1 Pet. 2:9)*

[34] *But if we walk in the light, as he is in the light, we have fellowship with one another, and the blood of Jesus, his Son, purifies us from all sin. (1 John 1:7)*

[35] *Whoever loves his brother lives in the light, and there is nothing in him to make him*

inheritance not only in its blessings (God's provision, protection, peace) but also in its nature (holiness, truth, righteousness, purity).

*of light.* The Kingdom of God is the region of light: His presence, purity, perfection, holiness, righteousness, perfect knowledge. There is no darkness there at all.

Paul now moves out of the language of prayer into that of direct theological statement as he describes the God who has brought His people out of darkness and into His light.

### 1:13-20. THE PREEMINENCE AND MAJESTY OF JESUS CHRIST, THE REDEEMER.

***13 For he has rescued us from the dominion of darkness and brought us into the kingdom of the Son he loves,***

Paul explains how God has qualified them for their participation in the kingdom of light. Verses 13-14 also serve as a transition to Paul's teaching concerning Jesus Christ, which is his purpose to set forth.

**he has rescued us.** God's salvation is a rescue operation: He rescued us from sin, bondage and eternal destruction. This is described as the work of the Father who did it through His Son (v. 14) and by His Spirit.
**rescued us.** Aorist tense refers to the time of conversion.
**rescued us from the dominion of darkness and brought us into the kingdom of the Son.** The words are used territorially: the regions where the power extends (cf. Acts 26:18[36]).
**darkness.** As contrasted with light (v. 12). This does not refer merely to Satan. Darkness is separation from God (who is Light) and abiding under His curse. Darkness is absence and alienation from God, ignorance, rebellion and destruction. The devil abides in "darkness" himself.
**brought us.** Greek = "translated." The word is strictly local in its meaning; a literal,

---

*stumble. (1 John 2:10)*
[36] *to open their eyes and turn them from darkness to light, and from the power of Satan to God, so that they may receive forgiveness of sins and a place among those who are sanctified by faith in me. (Acts 26:18)*

actual translation. The word occurs four other times in the New Testament: the steward being put out of his job (Luke 16:4), the removal of Saul from the kingdom (Acts 13:22), Paul turning away many people from worshipping the goddess (Acts 19:26) and of removing mountains (1 Cor. 13:2). In classical literature, the word is used to signify the deportation of a body of men and the removal of them to form a colony. The believers are not wandering exiles in search of a home; they were taken out of one territory and settled in another.

*brought us into the kingdom of the Son.* This does not refer exclusively to the future kingdom. It is a historical fact, realized at our conversion. The believer has experienced a change of kingdoms. This should affect every part of our lives. This is why the believer is holy: because he is a citizen of the kingdom characterized by holiness.

*the kingdom of the Son.* The kingdom which has Christ for its Head and Founder. He rules over it, determines its laws, regulates its activities, protects its subjects and crowns them with blessings! In contrast to the darkness, this is a kingdom of light.

*the Son he loves.* Greek = "the Son of His love." The Son upon whom His infinite love rests (Matt. 3:17; 17:5), and to whom, therefore, the kingdom is given (John 3:35[37]).

*14 in whom we have redemption, the forgiveness of sins.*

This was how God rescued us from captivity in darkness: through Jesus' redeeming death on the cross. Cf. Eph. 1:7.[38]

*in whom.* In Christ. Paul's focus moves from the Father to the Son.

*we have redemption.* This redemption prepares us for our inheritance (v. 12), removes us from the realm of darkness (v. 13), and is a continuous gift enjoyed by the believer. The verb is present tense: we have redemption as an abiding and permanent possession.

*redemption.* "Redemption" means that a captive is set free from bondage through the payment of a price. Through Jesus' blood we were delivered from bondage to: the penalty of sin, God's eternal wrath, having to

---

[37] *The Father loves the Son and has placed everything in his hands. (John 3:35)*

[38] *In him we have redemption through his blood, the forgiveness of sins, in accordance with the riches of God's grace (Eph. 1:7)*

obey the law for righteousness, the power of Satan. This is accomplished "through His blood" (NKJV[39]).

***the forgiveness of sins.*** In apposition with redemption. This is the special element of redemption. The forgiveness of sins makes all the other aspects of redemption possible.

The next verse begins a lofty and comprehensive description of the preeminence of Jesus Christ, the sweeping glory of His Person and work (vv. 15-20). No doubt these verses were composed in reference to the errors prevalent at Colosse. Paul states absolute truth that will stand in any context, but his thoughts are molded so as to bear against the false teachings which were in circulation. In this mighty torrent of passionate affirmation of Christ, Paul sweeps away every error regarding His preeminence and all-sufficiency. Leadership principle: it is not always necessary to deal directly with errors. Many times it's better to affirm positive truths than to become mired in point-by-point negative corrections. When banks train their new tellers, they teach them what real money looks and feels like, rather than attempting to teach them the specific details of every single counterfeit that has ever been made.

Jesus is described in His relation to God (v. 15a), the universe (vv. 15b-17) and to the church (vv. 18-20). This description draws together His work in creating, maintaining and redeeming the world. Such a task would take most men six volumes to accomplish; Paul does it in six verses!

**15 *He is the image of the invisible God, the firstborn over all creation.***

***He is.*** Essentially and permanently (John 1:1-3; 1 John 1:1). He was so before creation, He was so in His incarnation, and He will be so for eternity. He eternally "is" the image of the invisible God (John 8:58[40]).

***the image of the invisible God.*** "Image" here means more than "likeness," which can be incidental and superficial. Jesus is the exact and perfect representation and revelation of God (the "Logos" of God). He does not merely look like God; He embodies God, He is God. He is the very substance of God. Jesus is the visible manifestation of that in God which

---

[39] *in whom we have redemption through His blood, the forgiveness of sins. (Col 1:14, NKJV)*

[40] *"I tell you the truth," Jesus answered, "before Abraham was born, I am!"*

is otherwise invisible and incommunicable (Phil. 2:6[41]; Heb. 1:3[42]; John 1:18[43]; 14:9[44]; 2 Cor. 4:4[45]; 1 Tim. 3:16[46]). Jesus is the perfect and total expression of God, possessing all the elements and attributes of His nature. He is the complete and absolute manifestation of God. Only God Himself can fully reveal God. Jesus reveals more than the will of God or the character of God; He reveals the fullness of God (2:9). He is the visible image of the invisible God.

The universe, in contrast, only declares the power and glory of God (Rom. 1:20[47]; Ps. 19:1[48]); it does not embody it.

Created man reflects the image and likeness of God (1 Cor. 11:7[49]; Gen. 1:26-27; 9:6[50]; Jam. 3:9[51]), but is not one with Him. Man was only a faint and fractional representation of God even when he was first created, and now he is corrupted and defaced by sin.

---

[41] *Who, being in very nature God... (Phil. 2:6)*

[42] *The Son is the radiance of God's glory and the exact representation of his being... (Heb. 1:3)*

[43] *No one has ever seen God, but God the One and Only, who is at the Father's side, has made him known. (John 1:18)*

[44] *Jesus answered: "Don't you know me, Philip, even after I have been among you such a long time? Anyone who has seen me has seen the Father. How can you say, 'Show us the Father'?" (John 14:9)*

[45] *The god of this age has blinded the minds of unbelievers, so that they cannot see the light of the gospel of the glory of Christ, who is the image of God. (2 Cor. 4:4)*

[46] *And without controversy great is the mystery of godliness: God was manifested in the flesh, Justified in the Spirit, Seen by angels, Preached among the Gentiles, Believed on in the world, Received up in glory. (1 Tim. 3:16, NKJV)*

[47] *For since the creation of the world God's invisible qualities – his eternal power and divine nature – have been clearly seen, being understood from what has been made, so that men are without excuse. (Rom. 1:20)*

[48] *The heavens declare the glory of God; the skies proclaim the work of his hands. (Ps. 19:1)*

[49] *A man ought not to cover his head, since he is the image and glory of God; but the woman is the glory of man. (1 Cor. 11:7)*

[50] *...in the image of God has God made man. (Gen. 9:6)*

[51] *...men, who have been made in God's likeness. (James 3:9)*

***the invisible God.*** That God is "invisible" does not mean merely that He cannot be seen with the human eye, but that He is fundamentally unknowable by finite man. Cf. 1 Tim. 1:17[52]; Rom. 1:20[53]; Heb. 11:27[54]; Ex. 33:20[55]; 1 Tim. 6:16.[56] In the Lord Jesus, the unknowable God becomes known (1 John 1:1[57]).

***the firstborn over all creation.*** A description of Jesus' lordship over the universe. He is exalted above all. This statement does not make Him a part of the creation (since He created all things – v. 16 – and is Himself, therefore, uncreated), but the One who has sovereign dominion over it all (Heb. 1:2[58]; Ps. 89:27[59]).

***the firstborn.*** Paul uses the word without explanation, as one whose meaning was already known to the readers. The simplest meaning of "firstborn" in the OT is that of priority of birth. Thus, many heretics (e.g., the ancient Arians) have used this verse to promote the heresy that Jesus was created. But this cannot be the meaning here – as if Jesus were the first created of all things – since He was eternally uncreated (v. 17). Thus, the secondary and derived meaning of "firstborn" – a designation of dignity and precedence, implied by priority (e.g., Israel's election in Ex. 4:22[60];

---

[52] *Now to the King eternal, immortal, invisible, the only God, be honor and glory for ever and ever. Amen. (1 Tim. 1:17)*

[53] *For since the creation of the world God's invisible qualities – his eternal power and divine nature – have been clearly seen, being understood from what has been made, so that men are without excuse. (Rom. 1:20)*

[54] *By faith he left Egypt, not fearing the king's anger; he persevered because he saw him who is invisible. (Heb. 11:27)*

[55] *"But," he said, "you cannot see my face, for no one may see me and live." (Ex. 33:20)*

[56] *who alone is immortal and who lives in unapproachable light, whom no one has seen or can see. To him be honor and might forever. Amen. (1 Tim. 6:16)*

[57] *That which was from the beginning, which we have heard, which we have seen with our eyes, which we have looked at and our hands have touched – this we proclaim concerning the Word of life. (1 John 1:1)*

[58] *but in these last days he has spoken to us by his Son, whom he appointed heir of all things, and through whom he made the universe. (Heb. 1:2)*

[59] *I will also appoint him my firstborn, the most exalted of the kings of the earth. (Ps. 89:27)*

[60] *Then say to Pharaoh, 'This is what the Lord says: Israel is my firstborn son, (Ex. 4:22)*

Jer. 31:9[61]; Rom. 8:29[62]; Heb. 1:6[63]; 12:23[64]) – must be Paul's meaning. "Firstborn of all creation" does not mean that Jesus was ever created or "born" (with the exception of His physical human birth to Mary, Luke 2:7,[65] 22-23), as the ancient Arians and modern Jehovah's Witnesses assert, but refers to His rank, as compared with all creation, of firstborn in preeminence.

Paul's context for the use of this term was the Old Testament. In Israel, the firstborn son had special rights and privileges including a larger share of the inheritance. In Ex. 4:22[66] and Jer. 31:9,[67] the nation of Israel is called God's "firstborn," meaning that the nation was chosen by God to be the recipient of special privileges and blessings, as compared with the Gentile nations. This usage of the term "firstborn" as meaning the most illustrious of its class is found in other places. In Job 18:13[68] the "firstborn of death" is a deadly disease. In Is. 14:30[69] the "firstborn of the poor" means the poorest of the poor. In Ps. 89:27[70] "I will make Him my firstborn" means to invest Him with royal dignity, and clothe Him with preeminent splendor, so as to make Him exalted in majesty above all the kings of the earth.

---

[61] *...I am Israel's father, and Ephraim is my firstborn son. (Jer. 31:9)*
[62] *For those God foreknew he also predestined to be conformed to the likeness of his Son, that he might be the firstborn among many brothers. (Rom. 8:29)*
[63] *And again, when God brings his firstborn into the world, he says, "Let all God's angels worship him." (Heb. 1:6)*
[64] *to the church of the firstborn, whose names are written in heaven. You have come to God, the judge of all men, to the spirits of righteous men made perfect, (Heb. 12:23)*
[65] *and she gave birth to her firstborn, a son... (Luke 2:7)*
[66] *Then say to Pharaoh, 'This is what the Lord says: Israel is my firstborn son, (Ex. 4:22)*
[67] *They will come with weeping; they will pray as I bring them back. I will lead them beside streams of water on a level path where they will not stumble, because I am Israel's father, and Ephraim is my firstborn son. (Jer. 31:9)*
[68] *It (i.e., the sickness that comes upon the wicked) eats away parts of his skin; death's firstborn (i.e., the worst of sicknesses) devours his limbs. (Job 18:13)*
[69] *The firstborn of the poor will feed, And the needy will lie down in safety; I will kill your roots with famine, And it will slay your remnant. (Is. 14:30, NKJV)*
[70] *I will also appoint him my firstborn, the most exalted of the kings of the earth. (Ps. 89:27)*

This is the sense in which Christ is called the "firstborn." The term refers to His position, rank, rights and special privileges.

The expression "firstborn" here has no connection with the incorrect idea of Jesus being the "only begotten" Son of the Father (John 1:14, 18, KJV). If Jesus is "only begotten," how can He be "first-begotten"? In John 1:14[71] and 18,[72] "only begotten" should have been translated "unique" (cf. Paul's reference to Isaac in Heb. 11:17[73] where the same Greek word is also translated "only begotten" in the KJV, whereas Abraham had many sons, Gen. 25:6[74]).

***all creation.*** Includes everything and everyone in every realm (v. 16).

**16 For by him all things were created: things in heaven and on earth, visible and invisible, whether thrones or powers or rulers or authorities; all things were created by him and for him.**

***For.*** This gives the grounds for Jesus' lordship over all things (v. 15b). He is exalted and preeminent over all (i.e., He is "the Firstborn over all creation") because He created and sustains all things for His own purposes and glory.

***by him.*** Greek = "in Him." All things were created by Him and also "in Him": all things came to pass within the sphere of His purpose and are dependent upon Him.

***all things.*** Greek = "the all" – the whole universe. Without the article, it would be all things individually, not collectively.

***were created.*** Aorist tense. A definite historical event: the physical act of creation.

***visible and invisible.*** This does not refer to the earthly and heavenly realms, but to the physical and spiritual realms.

---

[71] *And the Word was made flesh, and dwelt among us, (and we beheld his glory, the glory as of the only begotten of the Father,) full of grace and truth. (John 1:14, KJV)*

[72] *No man hath seen God at any time; the only begotten Son, which is in the bosom of the Father, he hath declared him. (John 1:18, KJV)*

[73] *By faith Abraham, when he was tried, offered up Isaac: and he that had received the promises offered up his only begotten son. (Heb. 11:17, KJV)*

[74] *But while he was still living, he gave gifts to the sons of his concubines and sent them away from his son Isaac to the land of the east. (Gen. 25:6)*

**whether thrones or powers or rulers or authorities.** The entire heavenly hierarchy as well as the kingdom of darkness and the kingdoms of this world; includes all rulers and authorities in every realm. Jesus is the Creator of all of them; therefore, He is greater than all of them. Paul's purpose here, as elsewhere in his writings, is not to give a precise catalog of the ranks and places of each kind of political and spiritual authority. Cf. 2:10; Eph. 1:21[75]; 3:10; 6:12[76]; 1 Cor. 15:24[77]; Tit. 3:1.[78] Such verses assert the existence of different degrees, ranks and categories in the spiritual realm, but do not give their precise details. Paul does not promote an elaborate and exact angelology anywhere.

Paul aims at the angel worship of the Colossians here. Jesus is above all. When believers focus on angels and depend on them as mediators for their communion with God, they are degrading the Son of God who is above them all, and is the sole Mediator (cf. God's assessment of previous mediators in Matt. 17:5[79]; Ex. 24:2[80]). Today, the Christian must disallow all other mediators such as Mary and the saints, the infallible prophet or teacher of the Word whose tapes and books become the preeminent and authoritative source of truth, and the great "anointed" men and women who, with lightning coming out of their fingers, "impart" more of God to others (Paul and Barnabas refused this kind of depiction of themselves in Acts 14). Jesus is above all and He is equally

---

[75] *far above all rule and authority, power and dominion, and every title that can be given, not only in the present age but also in the one to come. (Eph. 1:21)*

[76] *For our struggle is not against flesh and blood, but against the rulers, against the authorities, against the powers of this dark world and against the spiritual forces of evil in the heavenly realms. (Eph. 6:12)*

[77] *Then the end will come, when he hands over the kingdom to God the Father after he has destroyed all dominion, authority and power. (1 Cor. 15:24)*

[78] *Remind the people to be subject to rulers and authorities, to be obedient, to be ready to do whatever is good, (Titus 3:1)*

[79] *While he was still speaking, a bright cloud enveloped them, and a voice from the cloud said, "This is my Son, whom I love; with him I am well pleased. Listen to him!" (Matt. 17:5)*

[80] *but Moses alone is to approach the Lord; the others must not come near. And the people may not come up with him. (Ex. 24:2)*

available to all believers. Why idolize the man of God, when we can worship God? We should not depend on others in any way as mediators between ourselves and God.

Moreover, every kind of authority – physical and spiritual – was created by Him and is therefore lesser than Him and subject to Him. All authorities owe their existence and authority to Him and should not be allowed to usurp His place of preeminence over all. This is why patriotic political change, for example, is not the purpose of the church, but constitutes a much lesser goal than our true goal – the exaltation of the Son of God who is above all authority. Any lesser "gospel" or Christian "purpose" is to be avoided.

Many claim that God is restoring such things as power, prophecy, holiness, church life, unity, etc. to the body of Christ. God's real purpose is to restore the lordship, preeminence and all-sufficiency of Jesus Christ to His body – and it is all in Him!

> ***all things.*** Repetition for emphasis. Collectively summing up. Cf. John 1:3.[81]
> ***all things were created by him and for him.*** All things had their beginning in Him, depend on Him for their continued existence and exist to serve Him and bring Him glory. Cf. Rom. 11:36[82]; 1 Cor. 8:6[83]; Heb. 2:10[84]; Eph. 1:10.[85] (This is no contradiction to verses such as Heb. 2:10[86] which

---

[81] *Through him all things were made; without him nothing was made that has been made. (John 1:3)*

[82] *For from him and through him and to him are all things. To him be the glory forever! Amen. (Rom. 11:36)*

[83] *yet for us there is but one God, the Father, from whom all things came and for whom we live; and there is but one Lord, Jesus Christ, through whom all things came and through whom we live. (1 Cor. 8:6)*

[84] *In bringing many sons to glory, it was fitting that God, for whom and through whom everything exists, should make the author of their salvation perfect through suffering. (Heb. 2:10)*

[85] *to be put into effect when the times will have reached their fulfillment – to bring all things in heaven and on earth together under one head, even Christ. (Eph. 1:10)*

[86] *In bringing many sons to glory, it was fitting that God, for whom and through whom*

present the Father as the Grounds and Purpose of all existence, since God is one and the Son of God fully embodies God's self-revelation and will for all creation.) The Son of God is the reason why creation exists at all, and why it is as it is. Jesus is not one of many good purposes – He is the only ultimate purpose of the universe. Moreover, He is not merely a part of creation. He is separate from and above all created things. The false teachers at Colosse proposed that the universe proceeded from God indirectly, through a succession of emanations. Christ, at best, was only one of them; thus, He was created and could not be the final purpose of the universe's existence.

**17 He is before all things, and in him all things hold together.**

**He is.** Speaks of Christ's absolute existence. Cf. Ex. 3:14[87]; John 8:58.[88] His is unchanging being. At every point of His existence it may be said of Him, "He is." "He" speaks of Jesus' personality; "is" refers to His eternal preexistence. "He is" is emphatic: He and no other.
**before all things.** In time.
**in him.** As in v. 16.
**in him all things hold together.** The Son of God not only created all things, but He preserves and maintains all things in continuous existence. He is the Giver and Sustainer of all life. He holds the universe together. Cf. Acts 17:28[89]; Heb. 1:3.[90] All things were created by Him, and all things (including the powers and authorities just mentioned in v. 16) are still held together by Him. No created being is autonomous. The Son of God is absolutely preeminent. Everything depends on Him for continued existence.

---

*everything exists, should make the author of their salvation perfect through suffering. (Heb. 2:10)*
[87] *God said to Moses, "I am who I am. This is what you are to say to the Israelites: 'I am has sent me to you.'" (Ex. 3:14)*
[88] *"I tell you the truth," Jesus answered, "before Abraham was born, I am!" (John 8:58)*
[89] *For in him we live and move and have our being... (Acts 17:28)*
[90] *The Son is the radiance of God's glory and the exact representation of his being, sustaining all things by his powerful word. After he had provided purification for sins, he sat down at the right hand of the Majesty in heaven. (Heb. 1:3)*

**18 And he is the head of the body, the church; he is the beginning and the firstborn from among the dead, so that in everything he might have the supremacy.**

*And he.* The same One who is before all things and by whom all things were created and are held together. Emphatic: He is the Head of the body, not any angels, created beings or religious leaders (e.g., the Pope or cult leaders). You have Him as the Head of the church; no replacements or supplements are necessary!

*the head of the body, the church.* The church is described as a body. In other places (e.g., Rom. 12:4; 1 Cor. 12:12-27), the image of a body is used to illustrate the functioning and interdependence of the members. Here it is used to emphasize the preeminence and authority of Christ as the Head of the church (cf. Eph. 1:22-23[91]; 5:23[92]). Also means that the church's life depends on its continued union with Him (cf. 2:19; Eph. 4:15-16[93]).

The church is a living organism, composed of members vitally united to each other, each member with his own place and function, each essential to the body's health, each dependent on the rest of the body for its life and well-being, while the whole organism and all the individual members derive their life from the Head and act under His guidance.

*the body, the church.* In apposition: the body is the church.

*he is the beginning.* This is the reason why He is the Head of the church: He is the beginning of the new spiritual life of His people. In Him the church begins (vv. 20-22). Through His death and resurrection, He is the Fount of all spiritual life and blessing.

---

[91] *And God placed all things under his feet and appointed him to be head over everything for the church, which is his body, the fullness of him who fills everything in every way. (Eph. 1:22-23)*

[92] *For the husband is the head of the wife as Christ is the head of the church, his body, of which he is the Savior. (Eph. 5:23)*

[93] *Instead, speaking the truth in love, we will in all things grow up into him who is the Head, that is, Christ. From him the whole body, joined and held together by every supporting ligament, grows and builds itself up in love, as each part does its work. (Eph 4:15-16)*

***the firstborn from among the dead.*** That Jesus is "the firstborn of the dead" means more than that He was the first to be physically resurrected from the dead (Acts 26:23[94]), never to die again (1 Cor. 15:20,[95] 23[96]; Rev. 1:5[97]; cf. John 11:44; Luke 7:15; 2 Kings 13:21); but the expression also refers to the fact that His resurrection has secured the resurrection and life of His people, and is both the pledge and the pattern of it. (See pp. 246-248 in *The Blood of God* by Malcolm Webber.) There is also a parallel between Jesus' preeminence over creation as the "firstborn over all creation" (v. 15) and His preeminence over the church as the firstborn from among the dead" (v. 18).

Thus, the expression "firstborn from among the dead" has a fourfold meaning. First, Jesus was the first to be resurrected from the dead with a glorified, spiritual body. Second, Jesus' resurrection is the guarantee of our future resurrections (1 Cor. 15:20). Third, His resurrection is the pattern that ours will follow (Phil. 3:21[98]; 1 John 3:2[99]; 1 Cor. 15:49[100]). Fourth, He is preeminent among all those who will be resurrected.

Some teachers have used the expression "firstborn from among the dead" to suggest that Jesus needed to be spiritually born again in His resurrection. One author wrote that to be born again is to "become a partaker of the divine

---

[94] *that the Christ would suffer and, as the first to rise from the dead, would proclaim light to his own people and to the Gentiles. (Acts 26:23)*

[95] *But Christ has indeed been raised from the dead, the firstfruits of those who have fallen asleep. (1 Cor. 15:20)*

[96] *But each in his own turn: Christ, the firstfruits; then, when he comes, those who belong to him. (1 Cor. 15:23)*

[97] *and from Jesus Christ, who is the faithful witness, the firstborn from the dead, and the ruler of the kings of the earth. To him who loves us and has freed us from our sins by his blood, (Rev. 1:5)*

[98] *who, by the power that enables him to bring everything under his control, will transform our lowly bodies so that they will be like his glorious body. (Phil. 3:21)*

[99] *Dear friends, now we are children of God, and what we will be has not yet been made known. But we know that when he appears, we shall be like him, for we shall see him as he is. (1 John 3:2)*

[100] *And just as we have borne the likeness of the earthly man, so shall we bear the likeness of the man from heaven. (1 Cor. 15:49)*

nature." The same author wrote that Jesus Christ was the first person ever to be born again. Therefore, in this author's understanding, Jesus became a partaker of the divine nature, which in turn means there was a time when Jesus was not a partaker of the divine nature. Thus, this false teaching actually denies the deity of Christ!

The Bible, however, teaches that Jesus' physical death redeemed us (1:22; Eph. 1:7[101]; etc.), He never died spiritually and His resurrection was a bodily one only (Rom. 8:11[102]; 1 Pet. 3:18[103]; 1 Cor. 15:20-23; Luke 24:36-46).

> *in everything.* In the universe and in the church.
> *he might have the supremacy.* Greek = "might become being first." As the Son of God He always was preeminent over all things. Through His life, death and resurrection He became the Head of the church.

**19 For God was pleased to have all his fullness dwell in him,**

This statement stands as a grand climax to the previous exalted descriptions of Christ.

> *For.* This verse, along with v. 20, shows how Christ was able to accomplish the great work described in v. 18. Since the fullness of God dwelt in the Son, reconciliation could be accomplished through the blood of His cross, with Him thereby becoming the Beginning of the church and the Head of the body. Thus, the efficacy of Christ's death is ascribed to His deity. Jesus' blood redeemed us because He was God; His physical death had infinite value and was sufficient to pay the penalty for all men (cf. 1:14-15; Heb.

---

[101] *In him we have redemption through his blood, the forgiveness of sins, in accordance with the riches of God's grace (Eph. 1:7)*

[102] *And if the Spirit of him who raised Jesus from the dead is living in you, he who raised Christ from the dead will also give life to your mortal bodies through his Spirit, who lives in you. (Rom. 8:11)*

[103] *For Christ died for sins once for all, the righteous for the unrighteous, to bring you to God. He was put to death in the body but made alive by the Spirit, (1 Pet. 3:18)*

9:13-15[104]; 1:3[105]; Acts 20:28[106]; 1 Cor. 2:8[107]; Zech. 13:7[108]; 12:1-10[109]; Acts 3:15[110]).

**God was pleased.** It was more than His will: God is "pleased" by this. The Father was pleased to make His Son preeminent; you should be too!

***all his fullness.*** The sum-total of the divine powers and attributes (2:9; Eph. 3:19[111]). The totality of God dwells in Him.

***dwell.*** Permanently. The Greek word expresses permanence rather than a temporary arrangement.

**20 and through him to reconcile to himself all things, whether things on earth or things in heaven, by making peace through his blood, shed on the cross.**

***through him.*** Reconciliation was through the One in whom all the fullness of God dwells. God was "pleased" to do this (v. 19).

***to reconcile to himself... by making peace.*** The reconciliation happened at the same time as the making of peace (cf. Eph. 2:15[112]).

---

[104] *For if the blood of bulls and goats and a heifer's ashes sprinkling those who are ceremonially unclean purifies them with physical cleansing, how much more surely will the blood of Christ, who with an eternal Spirit gave Himself a spotless offering to God, purify your consciences from works that mean mere death, to serve the ever living God? And this is why He is the Mediator of a new covenant... (Heb. 9:13-15, Williams New Testament)*

[105] *The Son is the radiance of God's glory and the exact representation of his being, sustaining all things by his powerful word. After he had provided purification for sins, he sat down at the right hand of the Majesty in heaven. (Heb. 1:3)*

[106] *... Be shepherds of the church of God, which he bought with his own blood. (Acts 20:28)*

[107] *None of the rulers of this age understood it, for if they had, they would not have crucified the Lord of glory. (1 Cor. 2:8)*

[108] *"Awake, O sword, against My Shepherd, Against the Man who is My Companion," Says the Lord of hosts. "Strike the Shepherd, And the sheep will be scattered; Then I will turn My hand against the little ones. (Zech. 13:7, NKJV)*

[109] *...saith the Lord ...they shall look upon me whom they have pierced... (Zech. 12:1-10, KJV)*

[110] *You killed the author of life, but God raised him from the dead. We are witnesses of this. (Acts 3:15)*

[111] *to know the love of Christ which passes knowledge; that you may be filled with all the fullness of God. (Eph. 3:19, NKJV)*

[112] *having abolished in His flesh the enmity, that is, the law of commandments contained*

**to himself.** "Reconciliation" implies previous estrangement. Sin had separated man from God and brought enmity between them. Now man can be reconciled to His Creator (cf. Rom. 5:10[113]; 2 Cor. 5:18[114]). Salvation involved God, and not the devil primarily.

**all things, whether things on earth or things in heaven.** Although not itself morally responsible, the whole universe was brought under the curse of sin when man fell (Rom. 8:20[115]; Job 15:15[116]), and through Jesus' death it will be cleansed and restored to the state of blessing which was God's original purpose for the world (Rom. 8:21[117]). This verse does not imply – as it has been used – that all sinful men and angels will ultimately be saved (Matt. 25:46[118]; Rev. 20:10[119]; etc).

**things on earth or things in heaven.** Man corrupted the earth by his sin; Satan corrupted the heavens by his sin.

**peace through his blood.** Through Jesus' physical death that paid the penalty for his sins, man can have peace with God (Eph. 2:12-18).

### 1:21-23. THE COLOSSIANS ARE INCLUDED IN THIS GLORIOUS RECONCILIATION IF THEY HOLD FAST TO THEIR FAITH.

Paul's thought now changes from Christ's preeminence to the Colossian Christians' standing before God. These two thoughts are directly related: the believer's position before God is dependent upon his continued faith in the preeminent Christ.

---

*in ordinances, so as to create in Himself one new man from the two, thus making peace,* (Eph. 2:15, NKJV)

[113] *For if, when we were God's enemies, we were reconciled to him through the death of his Son, how much more, having been reconciled, shall we be saved through his life!* (Rom. 5:10)

[114] *All this is from God, who reconciled us to himself through Christ and gave us the ministry of reconciliation:* (2 Cor. 5:18)

[115] *For the creation was subjected to futility, not willingly, but because of Him who subjected it in hope;* (Rom. 8:20, NKJV)

[116] *...even the heavens are not pure in his eyes,* (Job 15:15)

[117] *because the creation itself also will be delivered from the bondage of corruption into the glorious liberty of the children of God.* (Rom. 8:21, NKJV)

[118] *"Then they will go away to eternal punishment, but the righteous to eternal life."* (Matt. 25:46)

[119] *...They will be tormented day and night for ever and ever.* (Rev 20:10)

***21 Once you were alienated from God and were enemies in your minds because of your evil behavior.***

*alienated from God.* This is the condition of fallen, spiritually dead man. Cf. Eph. 4:18.[120]

*enemies.* We were active enemies to God.

*enemies in your minds.* Man's mind is the spiritual seat of his enmity against God.

*your evil behavior.* The outward manifestation of our enmity.

***22 But now he has reconciled you by Christ's physical body through death to present you holy in his sight, without blemish and free from accusation –***

*But now.* In contrast to the previous alienation.

*he.* The Father.

*reconciled.* Now the believer has right standing before God. Justification. Now!

*by Christ's physical body through death.* Jesus did not die spiritually. His physical death redeemed us.

Paul's emphasis on the death of Jesus' physical body underscores the historical and real nature of Jesus' death and therefore of God's reconciling grace. The Colossians are being captivated by abstract and esoteric beliefs (the "philosophy" of 2:8). Therefore, Paul insists that at the core of true faith are the historical realities of the gospel.

*to present you holy in his sight.* The purpose of His redeeming death: that we should be holy before God. In contrast to the former "evil behavior" of v. 21.

*holy.* Separate from sin and the world and unto God.

*in his sight.* At the time of the future judgment. Cf. v. 23: "if you continue…" Our final victorious presentation before God will depend upon our faithful

---

[120] *They are darkened in their understanding and separated from the life of God because of the ignorance that is in them due to the hardening of their hearts. (Eph. 4:18)*

endurance. Cf. Eph. 5:27 [121]; 1 Thess. 3:13.[122] Through Jesus' death, we will be holy before God!

**without blemish.** Cf. Eph. 1:4[123]; 5:27.

**free from accusation.** Not only free from actual blemishes, but from any charge of them.

**23 if you continue in your faith, established and firm, not moved from the hope held out in the gospel. This is the gospel that you heard and that has been proclaimed to every creature under heaven, and of which I, Paul, have become a servant.**

**if you continue in your faith.** Conditional. Cf. 1 Cor. 15:2[124]; Matt. 24:13.[125] The false teachers are trying to add spiritual "supplements" to the Colossians' faith. But the gospel needs no supplements and it is at the peril of their salvation if they lose hold of it. The "faith" they must "continue in" is the preeminence and all-sufficiency of Christ (vv. 15-19).

Paul did not teach a simplistic "once saved, always saved" Christianity (cf. Heb. 6:4-12; 10:26-39; John 15:1-6; 2 Pet. 2:20-22; 1 John 5:16), which produces a false security. However, neither did he teach the other extreme idea that the believer is lost every time he sins and has to be "resaved" continually, which produces anxiety and insecurity. True faith is an abiding and enduring relationship with God. As the believer abides in true relationship with God he is fully assured of his eternal salvation (John 6:39[126]; 10:28-29[127]).

---

[121] *and to present her to himself as a radiant church, without stain or wrinkle or any other blemish, but holy and blameless. (Eph. 5:27)*

[122] *May he strengthen your hearts so that you will be blameless and holy in the presence of our God and Father when our Lord Jesus comes with all his holy ones. (1 Thess. 3:13)*

[123] *For he chose us in him before the creation of the world to be holy and blameless in his sight. In love (Eph. 1:4)*

[124] *By this gospel you are saved, if you hold firmly to the word I preached to you. Otherwise, you have believed in vain. (1 Cor. 15:2)*

[125] *but he who stands firm to the end will be saved. (Matt. 24:13)*

[126] *And this is the will of him who sent me, that I shall lose none of all that he has given me, but raise them up at the last day. (John 6:39)*

[127] *I give them eternal life, and they shall never perish; no one can snatch them out of*

***your faith.*** In Christ.

***established.*** Supported by the foundation of the truth. Truth is not optional or merely a "good idea" for the believer.

***firm.*** The believers' inward strength that settles them.

***not moved.*** The present participle signifies continual shifting. This is the effect the false teachers are having on the Colossian believers (cf. Eph. 4:14[128]).

***the gospel that you heard and that has been proclaimed to every creature under heaven.*** The gospel you heard is the same that has gone everywhere. Paul confirms the truth of what they've heard and also its universality.

***proclaimed to every creature under heaven.*** Cf. Mark 16:15.[129]

***of which I, Paul, have become a servant.*** Cf. Eph. 3:7.[130] Paul's focus now shifts to his own ministry.

### 1:24-29. PAUL'S JOY AND SUFFERINGS AND THE PURPOSE OF HIS MINISTRY.

***24 Now I rejoice in what was suffered for you, and I fill up in my flesh what is still lacking in regard to Christ's afflictions, for the sake of his body, which is the church.***

***I rejoice in what was suffered for you.*** Paul does not express self-pity but rejoices in the midst of his sufferings that are on behalf of the believers (Matt. 5:10-12). The sufferings will result in eternal glory (Rom. 8:19-21; 2 Cor. 4:17[131]). Paul writes from prison (4:18).

---

*my hand. My Father, who has given them to me, is greater than all; no one can snatch them out of my Father's hand. (John 10:28-29)*

[128] *Then we will no longer be infants, tossed back and forth by the waves, and blown here and there by every wind of teaching and by the cunning and craftiness of men in their deceitful scheming. (Eph. 4:14)*

[129] *He said to them, "Go into all the world and preach the good news to all creation. (Mark 16:15)*

[130] *I became a servant of this gospel by the gift of God's grace given me through the working of his power. (Eph. 3:7)*

[131] *For our light and momentary troubles are achieving for us an eternal glory that far outweighs them all. (2 Cor. 4:17)*

***I fill up in my flesh what is still lacking in regard to Christ's afflictions.*** This does not refer to Christ's vicarious sufferings which are not "lacking" in any way (e.g., Heb. 10:12[132]) and which no man could ever enter into. (Medieval Catholics understood this clause as referring to the defects of the atonement, and that its defects may be compensated for by the sufferings of the saints; also thereby justifying such practices as indulgences.) These are the sufferings for Christ that are not endured by Him personally, but by His servants in all generations who carry out His work and who bear His reproach. Cf. 2 Cor. 1:5[133]; Phil. 3:10.[134] In that sense they are His afflictions. All the sufferings of Christ's body are Christ's own sufferings (Is. 63:9[135]; Acts 9:4[136]; 1 Cor. 8:12[137]; Matt. 25:40[138]; Acts 5:39[139]; Heb. 13:13[140]). Thus, His sufferings will not be complete until the end. Every suffering saint of God in every age is filling up the sufferings of Christ, and on behalf of His body. No suffering is in vain – it is all a part of the "filling up" of Christ's sufferings. This is the privilege of those who follow Jesus.

***I fill up.*** Present tense: "I am filling up."

***lacking.*** Greek = "behind."

---

[132] *But when this priest had offered for all time one sacrifice for sins, he sat down at the right hand of God. (Heb. 10:12)*

[133] *For just as the sufferings of Christ flow over into our lives, so also through Christ our comfort overflows. (2 Cor. 1:5)*

[134] *I want to know Christ and the power of his resurrection and the fellowship of sharing in his sufferings, becoming like him in his death, (Phil. 3:10)*

[135] *In all their distress he too was distressed, and the angel of his presence saved them. In his love and mercy he redeemed them; he lifted them up and carried them all the days of old. (Is. 63:9)*

[136] *He fell to the ground and heard a voice say to him, "Saul, Saul, why do you persecute me?" (Acts 9:4)*

[137] *When you sin against your brothers in this way and wound their weak conscience, you sin against Christ. (1 Cor. 8:12)*

[138] *"The King will reply, 'I tell you the truth, whatever you did for one of the least of these brothers of mine, you did for me.'" (Matt. 25:40)*

[139] *But if it is from God, you will not be able to stop these men; you will only find yourselves fighting against God." (Acts 5:39)*

[140] *Therefore let us go forth to Him, outside the camp, bearing His reproach. (Heb. 13:13, NKJV)*

***for the sake of his body, which is the church.*** Paul is suffering for the salvation and maturity of the church.

**25 I have become its servant by the commission God gave me to present to you the word of God in its fullness –**

***its servant.*** The servant of the church (returns to his thought of v. 23). Paul did not use the people of God for his own self-serving agendas. He truly served the church.
***commission.*** Greek = "stewardship." Cf. 1 Cor. 9:17[141]; 4:1[142]; Eph. 3:2.[143]
***to present to you the word of God in its fullness.*** Greek = "to fulfill the Word of God." Cf. Rom. 15:19.[144] To fulfill the duty of stewardship, in doing all that this preaching of the Word requires.

**26 the mystery that has been kept hidden for ages and generations, but is now disclosed to the saints.**

***the mystery.*** This refers to the admission of the Gentiles to the privileges of covenant relationship with God (cf. v. 27; Eph. 3:6[145]). This is the word Paul preaches.
***the saints.*** All the saints.

In the Old Testament, Israel was to be God's "own possession" among all peoples. She would be His own redeemed people. This relationship was not offered to any other nation in Old Testament times (Ps. 147:19-20; Ex. 19:5-6; Lev. 20:24, 26; Deut. 4:8; 7:6-8; 10:14-15; 14:2; 2 Sam. 7:23; 1 Kings 8:53; 1

---

[141] *If I preach voluntarily, I have a reward; if not voluntarily, I am simply discharging the trust committed to me. (1 Cor. 9:17)*
[142] *So then, men ought to regard us as servants of Christ and as those entrusted with the secret things of God. (1 Cor. 4:1)*
[143] *Surely you have heard about the administration of God's grace that was given to me for you, (Eph. 3:2)*
[144] *by the power of signs and miracles, through the power of the Spirit. So from Jerusalem all the way around to Illyricum, I have fully proclaimed the gospel of Christ. (Rom. 15:19)*
[145] *This mystery is that through the gospel the Gentiles are heirs together with Israel, members together of one body, and sharers together in the promise in Christ Jesus. (Eph. 3:6)*

Chron. 17:21; Amos 3:2; John 4:22; Eph. 2:12, 19). There were individuals in the Old Testament who were not from Israel, yet received salvation (cf. Luke 4:25-27). Furthermore, the Old Testament did foretell the coming time when salvation would be offered to all nations (e.g., Gen. 12:3; 22:18; 26:4; 28:14; Ps. 67; 72:17; Is. 11:10; Joel 2:28; Amos 9:11-12; Hab. 2:14; Gal. 3:8). Nevertheless, prior to Jesus' coming, salvation was only specifically offered to Israel (Eph. 2:11-19; 3:3-9). There was no "Great Commission" responsibility given to Israel to preach the Word of God to the nations – it was a "mystery" that the Gentiles would one day enter God's covenant.

**27 To them God has chosen to make known among the Gentiles the glorious riches of this mystery, which is Christ in you, the hope of glory.**

- **has chosen to make known.** Greek = "willed to make known." The salvation of the Gentiles was part of the eternal purpose of God, not just a spontaneous "add-in" part of His plan when Israel rejected her Messiah (Eph. 3:4-11).
- **the glorious riches.** Greek = "the richness of the glory." The expression does not mean the glorious riches, but rather how rich is the glory. Already the Gentiles can know of the glory of God.
- **which is.** This is the essence of the mystery itself, the heart of our covenant with God: Christ dwelling in our hearts (Eph. 3:17[146]; Gal. 2:20[147]).
- **Christ.** Himself, not only His power, doctrine, ethics, character, moral code or holiness. This is Paul's point in Colossians: the preeminence and all-sufficiency of Christ Himself.
- **you.** The Colossian believers were mostly Gentiles.
- **Christ in you.** Not only are we "in Christ," but Christ is also "in us." In this union with Him, we participate not only in His sufferings but also in His fellowship and His glory.
- **the hope of glory.** Greek = "the hope of the glory." They already have a measure of glory now, but the full inheritance of glory will come

---

[146] *so that Christ may dwell in your hearts through faith. And I pray that you, being rooted and established in love, (Eph. 3:17)*

[147] *I have been crucified with Christ and I no longer live, but Christ lives in me. The life I live in the body, I live by faith in the Son of God, who loved me and gave himself for me. (Gal. 2:20)*

at Jesus' return (John 17:20-24; Rom. 8:17-18[148]). This is a quick summary of both the nature and goal of the gospel: "Christ in you, the hope of glory."

**28 We proclaim him, admonishing and teaching everyone with all wisdom, so that we may present everyone perfect in Christ.**

*We proclaim him.* The Son of God is the content of our message – Him first, Him last, Him in the midst. In contrast to the false teachers. We proclaim Him – not other things. Union with Jesus is not merely a peripheral issue – it is our only message. When God has given you a diamond, why go after dirt?

*admonishing and teaching.* Both negative and positive aspects of his ministry.

*admonishing.* Greek = "warning."

*everyone with all wisdom, so that we may present everyone perfect.* "Every" is stated three times to emphasize the universality of the gospel against the spiritual exclusiveness encouraged by the false teachers.

*with all wisdom.* In every form of wisdom. No fifteen-minute "seeker-friendly" sermonette here! This opposed the idea of the esoteric and exotic wisdom promoted by the false teachers: higher knowledge for the few select ones and just the simple basics for the masses. In true Christianity, the highest wisdom is freely open to all (cf. 2:2-3). Paul's goal is that every believer be instructed in the whole of Christian wisdom.

*present.* Cf. v. 22.

*perfect.* Mature. Paul's goal is that every believer comes to spiritual maturity.

Paul's purpose was not to build a ministry or start an organization. Neither was his goal to change the government, Christianize the culture or reform society. His purpose was to build the Bride of Christ to maturity. The measure of this maturity is full union with Christ (v. 27; Eph. 4:13[149]: 5:25-27). This

---

[148] *Now if we are children, then we are heirs – heirs of God and co-heirs with Christ, if indeed we share in his sufferings in order that we may also share in his glory. I consider that our present sufferings are not worth comparing with the glory that will be revealed in us. (Rom. 8:17-18)*

[149] *until we all reach unity in the faith and in the knowledge of the Son of God and become mature, attaining to the whole measure of the fullness of Christ. (Eph. 4:13)*

union will be accomplished through the ministry of the Word of God by the Holy Spirit. This was Paul's single purpose in everything he did; it should be our purpose in all we do.

Notice also how that in the midst of the Colossians' struggles, faults and errors, Paul still had a great vision for the accomplishment of God's ultimate purposes in their midst. He had not given up on them.

**29 To this end I labor, struggling with all his energy, which so powerfully works in me.**

*To this end.* The maturity of the Bride of Christ. Leadership principle: it is not enough for a leader merely to teach and preach; he must also travail in prayer for those to whom he ministers. Leaders not only teach; they also travail. This is the source of their power (Acts 6:4[150]).

*I labor.* Greek = "I also labor." Adds a new dimension of Paul's ministry beyond the warning and teaching just mentioned. Refers to his intercessory prayer on their behalf. This thought continues in 2:1ff.

*labor.* To toil to the point of weariness (Luke 5:5[151]).

*struggling.* The battle of prayer under the image of a contest or conflict of some kind. Cf. 1 Tim. 6:12[152]; 2 Tim. 4:7[153]; 1 Cor. 9:25[154]; 1 Thess. 2:2.[155]

*with all his energy.* The ministry of the Holy Spirit in Paul (Phil. 4:13[156]). He did not labor according to his own strength.

*works.* Greek word is used only of superhuman energy, good or evil.

---

[150] [we] will give our attention to prayer and the ministry of the word. (Acts 6:4)

[151] Simon answered, "Master, we've worked hard all night and haven't caught anything. But because you say so, I will let down the nets." (Luke 5:5)

[152] Fight the good fight of the faith. Take hold of the eternal life to which you were called when you made your good confession in the presence of many witnesses. (1 Tim. 6:12)

[153] I have fought the good fight, I have finished the race, I have kept the faith. (2 Tim. 4:7)

[154] Everyone who competes in the games goes into strict training. They do it to get a crown that will not last; but we do it to get a crown that will last forever. (1 Cor. 9:25)

[155] We had previously suffered and been insulted in Philippi, as you know, but with the help of our God we dared to tell you his gospel in spite of strong opposition. (1 Thess. 2:2)

[156] I can do everything through him who gives me strength. (Phil. 4:13)

## 2:1-3. PAUL'S PRAYER FOR THE COLOSSIANS.

***2:1 I want you to know how much I am struggling for you and for those at Laodicea, and for all who have not met me personally.***

*I want you to know.* Greek = "For I want you to know." Verse 1 follows on from 1:29.
*how much I am struggling for you.* Paul's conflict in prayer (cf. 4:12; Gal. 4:19[157]; John 11:33[158], 35[159], 38[160]).
*and for those at Laodicea.* Who probably were in the same danger of being led astray (4:16).
*and for all who have not met me personally.* These words show Paul must have been writing about prayer since it could not have involved his personal ministry. Also indicates that the Colossians and Laodicaeans were both personally unmet by Paul.

***2 My purpose is that they may be encouraged in heart and united in love, so that they may have the full riches of complete understanding, in order that they may know the mystery of God, namely, Christ,***

*My purpose.* This is the intent of Paul's prayer. The context is 1:28-29 (cf. Rom. 8:17-27).
*encouraged in heart.* Not only comforted (as is necessary in time of suffering and trial) but strengthened – to be firm in the faith and to resist the errors.
*united in love.* The result of embracing error is division in the body; thus, their union in love will be a safeguard against it. "Doctrine" does not divide; error divides.
*know.* Greek = "thorough knowledge."

---

[157] *My little children, of whom I travail in birth again until Christ be formed in you,* (Gal. 4:19, KJV)
[158] *Therefore, when Jesus saw her weeping, and the Jews who came with her weeping, He groaned in the spirit and was troubled.* (John 11:33, NKJV)
[159] *Jesus wept.* (John 11:35)
[160] *Then Jesus, again groaning in Himself, came to the tomb. It was a cave, and a stone lay against it.* (John 11:38, NKJV)

***namely, Christ.*** Christ Himself is the mystery of God (1:27; 1 Tim. 3:16[161]).

"Encouraged in heart": internally strengthened. "United in love": externally united. Cf. v. 5.

**3 in whom are hidden all the treasures of wisdom and knowledge.**

***in whom.*** In Christ.
***are hidden.*** They do not lie on the surface. They must be sought for earnestly, as men search for hidden treasure. Nevertheless, these mysteries are revealed in the preaching of the gospel (v. 2).
***all the treasures of wisdom and knowledge.*** The false teachers are offering them knowledge from sources other than Christ. In contradiction, Paul insists that the fullness of understanding is found in the knowledge of the mystery of God, which is the personal knowledge of Christ alone. Stresses His absolute all-sufficiency. Any search for truth or wisdom outside of Christ is doomed to failure.

Are you seeking knowledge and understanding, like the Colossians were? Jesus is the Truth (John 14:6[162]). If Jesus were merely "true" then He would conform to some higher standard of truth. However, Jesus Himself is "Truth": He Himself is the final and ultimate Standard of Truth by which everything else must be judged. Jesus Himself – His Person – is Truth.

Therefore, you can never come to any knowledge of Truth apart from knowing Him. In Him personally, in His Person, in Him "are hidden all the treasures of wisdom and knowledge." Only through the apprehension of Jesus – in experienced union and communion – will these treasures ever be revealed.

---

[161] *And without controversy great is the mystery of godliness: God was manifested in the flesh, Justified in the Spirit, Seen by angels, Preached among the Gentiles, Believed on in the world, Received up in glory. (1 Tim. 3:16, NKJV)*

[162] *Jesus answered, "I am the way and the truth and the life. No one comes to the Father except through me. (John 14:6)*

### 2:4-23. PAUL'S WARNING AGAINST THE FALSE TEACHINGS WHICH WILL LEAD THEM AWAY FROM CHRIST.
#### VV. 4-7. EXHORTATION TO ABIDE IN CHRIST.
#### VV. 8-15. GENERAL WARNING AGAINST THE FALSE TEACHINGS.
#### VV. 16-23. SPECIFIC WARNINGS AGAINST THE FALSE TEACHINGS.

*4 I tell you this so that no one may deceive you by fine-sounding arguments.*

*I tell you this.* Vv. 1-3. Paul has been commissioned by God to give the Gentiles the true gospel and he wars in prayer for them. Therefore, they should believe his teaching rather than that of the false teachers.

*fine-sounding.* Persuasive. You do not counterfeit a $3 bill! The false teachers are attempting to deceive by false reasoning. They are deceivers, con artists who use smooth talk to deceive the immature.

Paul is not against learning or developing good arguments per se, but he is against using one's learning and arguments to advance falsehoods. The motive behind the false teachers was not the true love of wisdom but the love of folly. Their speculations were baseless, existing in a false land that they themselves had created. The truths of the gospel were too tame for them, so they invented a new and exotic wisdom for themselves.

*5 For though I am absent from you in body, I am present with you in spirit and delight to see how orderly you are and how firm your faith in Christ is.*

In the midst of Paul's correction, some strong affirmation.

*though I am absent from you in body, I am present with you in spirit.* Probably does not refer to the Holy Spirit, but Paul's own spirit. Refers to Paul's own personal authority – as if he were present. Cf. 1 Cor. 5:3-4.[163] Affirms his apostolic connection with the church here.

---

[163] *Even though I am not physically present, I am with you in spirit. And I have already passed judgment on the one who did this, just as if I were present. When you are assembled in the name of our Lord Jesus and I am with you in spirit, and the power of our Lord Jesus is present, (1 Cor. 5:3-4)*

***how orderly you are.*** A military metaphor. The orderly arrangement of a harmonized and undivided church. Their external appearance.
***how firm your faith in Christ is.*** The internal reality of their lives which produced the outward orderliness. Cf. v. 2. Without internal commitment there is disorder in the church.
***firm.*** Means solid.

**6 So then, just as you received Christ Jesus as Lord, continue to live in him,**

A summary statement of Paul's message to the Colossians (cf. 1:28). Stay with Jesus Christ! Don't be moved away by the false teachers.

***you received.*** From Epaphras and the other teachers. It is scriptural to speak of "receiving Christ" (cf. John 1:12[164]). We "receive" Christ; we do not "accept" Him; He "accepts" us!
***Christ Jesus as Lord.*** Greek = "the Christ, Jesus, the Lord." The believer receives not only the doctrine of Christ, but Christ Himself (1:27; John 17:3[165]; Phil. 3:8[166]). Christ Himself dwells in the heart of the believer. Not merely intellectual affirmation of His lordship, but submission to that lordship.
***continue.*** Carry on your life in Him. Our salvation is gained *and* maintained only through Him. Abide in Him!

**7 rooted and built up in him, strengthened in the faith as you were taught, and overflowing with thankfulness.**

***rooted and built up in him.*** Two images: Jesus is both the soil and the foundation. Tenses are different: "rooted" is past, "being built up" (Greek) is present.

---

[164] *Yet to all who received him, to those who believed in his name, he gave the right to become children of God (John 1:12)*
[165] *Now this is eternal life: that they may know you, the only true God, and Jesus Christ, whom you have sent. (John 17:3)*
[166] *What is more, I consider everything a loss compared to the surpassing greatness of knowing Christ Jesus my Lord, for whose sake I have lost all things. I consider them rubbish, that I may gain Christ (Phil. 3:8)*

***in him.*** Not "on Him" but "in Him." Christ is the sphere within which the building takes place (Eph. 2:21[167]). Stresses: abide in Him!
***strengthened.*** Greek = "being strengthened."
***as you were taught.*** Stay with the gospel you first received.
***with thankfulness.*** There is much in this letter regarding thankfulness. Thankfulness is a preservative against these false doctrines since it keeps Christ in His proper place.

## 2:8-15. GENERAL WARNING AGAINST THE FALSE TEACHINGS.

Paul once again begins to attack the influence of the false teachers. The decisive attack will come in vv. 16-23. He gives the essential basis for it in vv. 9-10.

***8 See to it that no one takes you captive through hollow and deceptive philosophy, which depends on human tradition and the basic principles of this world rather than on Christ.***

***See to it.*** You do this! Paul is deeply concerned that they are giving place to the errors. It was their responsibility to keep themselves free from error; they were not to be dependent on Paul for this. A healthy church takes responsibility for its own doctrine.
***no one takes you captive.*** Very strong expression in Greek. The aim of the false teachers is to capture you and take you off as booty.
***through.*** How they are trying to do it.
***hollow and deceptive philosophy.*** Greek = "his philosophy and vain deceit." The vain deceit is explanatory of the philosophy. Paul is referring to the vain speculation of the false teachers, that threatens to undermine the faith of the church.
***which depends on human tradition.*** The source of the vain and deceptive teachings: the traditions of men (a mixture of Judaic [not Mosaic, biblical truth but supplemental Judaic traditions], Greek and Oriental traditions, which afterward developed into Gnosticism), and not the authority of the Scriptures.

---

[167] *In him the whole building is joined together and rises to become a holy temple in the Lord. (Eph. 2:21)*

*the basic principles of this world.* Greek = "rudiments of the world." Rudimentary teachings such as ceremonial rituals (meats, drinks, washings), asceticism, and secret mysteries. These all have the appearance of deep and higher realms of truth, but in reality, they are basic and earthly – weak and miserable, carnal and worldly, sensuous and mundane. Cf. Gal. 4:9.[168] They cannot be compared with the true spiritual glories of Christ. E.g., Buddhism (with their chanting and banging gongs), New Age "channeling," meditations and use of crystals, Catholic idols, rituals and sacraments (appealing to many because of their apparent "spirituality"), Orthodox icons, Charismatic obsession with angels and "anointed" men and women. We, on the other hand, can know and walk with God! Therefore how pathetic it is when these beggarly human traditions infiltrate the church! It is a return to bondage and not liberty in Christ (Gal. 4: 3[169])!

*rather than on Christ.* The false teachings are not founded in the teachings of the Bible, nor do they point to the Person of the Lord Jesus. He alone is the true Rule of all knowledge and wisdom; therefore, every true philosophy must begin and end with Him.

**9 *For in Christ all the fullness of the Deity lives in bodily form,***

This is what the believer has in Christ: the fullness of God! Don't give this up for the pathetic nonsense of men!

*For.* All true philosophy is in Christ, because in Him dwells all the fullness of the Godhead bodily. Any system not after Christ is worldly and wrong.

*in Christ.* Emphatic. In Him and in Him alone.

*all the fullness.* All of God is in Jesus.

*the fullness of the Deity.* The creation only reveals the attributes, majesty and

---

[168] *But now that you know God – or rather are known by God – how is it that you are turning back to those weak and miserable principles? Do you wish to be enslaved by them all over again? (Gal. 4:9)*

[169] *So also, when we were children, we were in slavery under the basic principles of the world. (Gal. 4:3)*

glory of God (Rom. 1:20[170]), but Jesus reveals His essential and personal nature. Jesus is the fullness of God Himself.

**the Deity.** Greek = "the Godhead."

**lives.** Greek = "dwells." The fullness of the Godhead eternally dwells in Christ: before His incarnation, during His incarnation in His humanity, and after His ascension in His glorified humanity. In the Son of God dwells the fullness of God – from eternity to eternity.

**in bodily form.** The fullness of God dwells in Him bodily since the time of the incarnation and to eternity (John 14:9[171]; etc.). In this context, Paul primarily refers to Christ's glorified state. This is a powerful affirmation of the eternal union of humanity with deity in Jesus Christ.

This is a powerful contrast to the false teachings – the human traditions and the rudiments of this world – with their angelic mediators separating man from God, and their miserable depictions of spirituality.

**10 and you have been given fullness in Christ, who is the head over every power and authority.**

This crowns Paul's argument. You have everything in Christ, so stay with Him!

**and you have been given fullness in Christ.** Greek = "you are in Him, made full." In Christ is the fullness of God, and, in Him, you have been given Christ's fullness! (Cf. John 1:16[172]; Eph. 1:23[173]; 3:19[174]; 4:13.[175])

---

[170] *For since the creation of the world God's invisible qualities – his eternal power and divine nature – have been clearly seen, being understood from what has been made, so that men are without excuse. (Rom. 1:20)*

[171] *Jesus answered: "Don't you know me, Philip, even after I have been among you such a long time? Anyone who has seen me has seen the Father. How can you say, 'Show us the Father'? (John 14:9)*

[172] *From the fullness of his grace we have all received one blessing after another. (John 1:16)*

[173] *which is his body, the fullness of him who fills everything in every way. (Eph. 1:23)*

[174] *and to know this love that surpasses knowledge – that you may be filled to the measure of all the fullness of God. (Eph. 3:19)*

[175] *until we all reach unity in the faith and in the knowledge of the Son of God and become mature, attaining to the whole measure of the fullness of Christ. (Eph. 4:13)*

> ***have been.*** Already! It's done.
> ***fullness.*** Therefore you do not need any supplementary sources of grace or truth, such as the false teachers are directing you to. Jesus is full of grace and truth (John 1:14[176]) and He has given us this fullness (John 1:16-17[177]).
> ***in Christ.*** You have everything you need and it is all in Christ.
> ***who is the head over every power and authority.*** He is the Head of all authorities (including angelic); therefore, do not become entangled with them.

**11 In him you were also circumcised, in the putting off of the sinful nature, not with a circumcision done by the hands of men but with the circumcision done by Christ,**

Neither do you need the rite of circumcision (or any other ritual) to make you complete, since you have already received in Christ the spiritual substance, of which that rite is but the shadow.

> ***you were also circumcised.*** Aorist tense shows a definite historical fact. You were circumcised!
> ***the putting off.*** A strong expression that signifies the idea of getting out of one's clothes and then getting away from them. The entire putting away of the old nature and life. Cf. 3:9-10.
> ***the sinful nature.*** The old man (Gal. 5:24[178]; Rom. 7:5[179]).
> ***not with a circumcision done by the hands of men.*** In itself ineffective to deal with the sinful nature (Eph. 2:11[180]).

---

[176] *The Word became flesh and made his dwelling among us. We have seen his glory, the glory of the One and Only, who came from the Father, full of grace and truth. (John 1:14)*

[177] *From the fullness of his grace we have all received one blessing after another. For the law was given through Moses; grace and truth came through Jesus Christ. (John 1:16-17)*

[178] *Those who belong to Christ Jesus have crucified the sinful nature with its passions and desires. (Gal. 5:24)*

[179] *For when we were controlled by the sinful nature, the sinful passions aroused by the law were at work in our bodies, so that we bore fruit for death. (Rom. 7:5)*

[180] *Therefore, remember that formerly you who are Gentiles by birth and called "uncircumcised" by those who call themselves "the circumcision" (that done in the body*

It is possible that the false teachers promoted circumcision to the Gentile Colossians, not as indispensable to salvation, in which case Paul would have definitely attacked them on this point (cf. Galatians), but as conferring a higher level of holiness. In many ways, this is a more subtle and dangerous heresy.

***the circumcision done by Christ.*** This circumcision is brought about by union with Christ. It is the true spiritual circumcision of the heart (Phil. 3:3[181]; Rom. 2:29[182]; Deut. 10:16[183]; 30:6[184]; Jer. 4:4[185]). In fleshly circumcision, only a portion of the body is removed. In true spiritual circumcision, through Christ, the entire corrupt and sinful nature is put away like a garment that is taken off and cast aside. Thus, the Holy Spirit and not formal religious ceremony is the agent of God's transforming power.

**12 having been buried with him in baptism and raised with him through your faith in the power of God, who raised him from the dead.**

The spiritual circumcision took place at the time of conversion, which is signified by water baptism (Rom. 6:4[186]).

---

*by the hands of men) – (Eph. 2:11)*

[181] *For it is we who are the circumcision, we who worship by the Spirit of God, who glory in Christ Jesus, and who put no confidence in the flesh (Phil. 3:3)*

[182] *No, a man is a Jew if he is one inwardly; and circumcision is circumcision of the heart, by the Spirit, not by the written code. Such a man's praise is not from men, but from God. (Rom. 2:29)*

[183] *Circumcise your hearts, therefore, and do not be stiff-necked any longer. (Deut. 10:16)*

[184] *The Lord your God will circumcise your hearts and the hearts of your descendants, so that you may love him with all your heart and with all your soul, and live. (Deut. 30:6)*

[185] *Circumcise yourselves to the Lord, circumcise your hearts, you men of Judah and people of Jerusalem, or my wrath will break out and burn like fire because of the evil you have done – burn with no one to quench it. (Jer. 4:4)*

[186] *We were therefore buried with him through baptism into death in order that, just as Christ was raised from the dead through the glory of the Father, we too may live a new life. (Rom. 6:4)*

***been buried with him in baptism and raised with him.*** Baptism signifies death, burial and resurrection.
***baptism.*** Greek = "the baptism."
***raised with him.*** To new life (Rom. 6:5-13). Not physically yet, but spiritually.
***through your faith.*** Your faith effected this; not the baptism itself (1 Pet. 3:21[187]).
***the power of God, who raised him from the dead.*** Cf. Rom. 8:11[188]; Eph. 1:19-20.[189] The power of God revealed in Jesus' resurrection is not only a pledge of the same physical power to be exerted in us in our future resurrection, but it is also already at work in us spiritually.

**13 When you were dead in your sins and in the uncircumcision of your sinful nature, God made you alive with Christ. He forgave us all our sins,**

***dead in your sins.*** Spiritual death (Eph. 2:1[190], 5[191]). You were dead to God and to all that His life produces in man – holiness, righteousness, truth, etc. Spiritual death means alienation from God.
***the uncircumcision of your sinful nature.*** Spiritually speaking; you may have been physically circumcised but your spiritual nature was uncircumcised.
***God made you alive with Christ.*** Alive to God (Rom. 6:11[192]; Eph. 2:5[193]).

---

[187] *and this water symbolizes baptism that now saves you also – not the removal of dirt from the body but the pledge of a good conscience toward God. It saves you by the resurrection of Jesus Christ,* (1 Pet. 3:21)

[188] *And if the Spirit of him who raised Jesus from the dead is living in you, he who raised Christ from the dead will also give life to your mortal bodies through his Spirit, who lives in you.* (Rom. 8:11)

[189] *and his incomparably great power for us who believe. That power is like the working of his mighty strength, which he exerted in Christ when he raised him from the dead and seated him at his right hand in the heavenly realms,* (Eph 1:19-20)

[190] *As for you, you were dead in your transgressions and sins,* (Eph. 2:1)

[191] *made us alive with Christ even when we were dead in transgressions – it is by grace you have been saved.* (Eph. 2:5)

[192] *In the same way, count yourselves dead to sin but alive to God in Christ Jesus.* (Rom. 6:11)

[193] *made us alive with Christ even when we were dead in transgressions – it is by grace you have been saved.* (Eph. 2:5)

***He forgave us all our sins.*** Freely! Cf. 2 Cor. 5:19[194]; Eph. 4:32.[195] It's done – apart from repentance and faith in Christ, we need nothing else to find peace with God.

***us.*** Paul includes himself and all believers.

**14 having canceled the written code, with its regulations, that was against us and that stood opposed to us; he took it away, nailing it to the cross.**

***canceled.*** Greek = "blotting out completely." The figure is the erasure of handwriting. This is the ground for the forgiveness of our sins.

***the written code.*** The law. However, since Paul says this law was against both Jew and Gentile, he means it with a wider reference: the moral law of God in general, of which the Mosaic Law was the chief representation. Only Israel was given the Mosaic Law (Deut. 4:8[196]; Ps. 147:19-20[197]; Eph. 2:12[198]).

***that was against us and that stood opposed to us.*** The moral law of God was good in itself (Rom. 7:12[199]), but fallen man could not keep it and thereby earn righteousness before God (Rom. 4:15[200]; 8:3[201]; 5:20[202];

---

[194] *that God was reconciling the world to himself in Christ, not counting men's sins against them. And he has committed to us the message of reconciliation. (2 Cor. 5:19)*

[195] *Be kind and compassionate to one another, forgiving each other, just as in Christ God forgave you. (Eph. 4:32)*

[196] *And what other nation is so great as to have such righteous decrees and laws as this body of laws I am setting before you today? (Deut. 4:8)*

[197] *He has revealed his word to Jacob, his laws and decrees to Israel. He has done this for no other nation; they do not know his laws. Praise the Lord. (Ps. 147:19-20)*

[198] *remember that at that time you were separate from Christ, excluded from citizenship in Israel and foreigners to the covenants of the promise, without hope and without God in the world. (Eph. 2:12)*

[199] *So then, the law is holy, and the commandment is holy, righteous and good. (Rom. 7:12)*

[200] *because law brings wrath. And where there is no law there is no transgression. (Rom. 4:15)*

[201] *For what the law was powerless to do in that it was weakened by the sinful nature, God did by sending his own Son in the likeness of sinful man to be a sin offering. And so he condemned sin in sinful man, (Rom. 8:3)*

[202] *The law was added so that the trespass might increase. But where sin increased, grace increased all the more, (Rom. 5:20)*

1 Cor. 15:56[203]; Gal. 3:23[204]). Thus, the law was "opposed" to us. The moral law is not "bad," but it is "against" fallen man and it cannot help him. It only reveals his sin and guilt to him, accusing him of sin and avenging his iniquity. The law has always been hostile to you: don't go back under its forms or any part of it now (Jam. 2:10[205])!

**us.** Both Jew and Gentile.

**he took it away.** Greek = "out of the midst." The law with its moral demands was abolished in Christ's death, as if crucified with Him. It is no longer "in the midst," in the foreground, as debtor's obligation is constantly before him, accusing him.

**nailing it to the cross.** When Jesus died on the cross, the law was abolished (Eph. 2:15[206]), since He fulfilled it by bearing its curse (Gal. 3:13[207]).

**15 And having disarmed the powers and authorities, he made a public spectacle of them, triumphing over them by the cross.**

Needless to say, this verse contains absolutely no reference to some fanciful battle in hell which Jesus had to win to conquer the devil, according to the teachings of some. God, the infinite Creator of all things, commands Satan, He does not fight with him.

Jesus' death on the cross disarmed Satan by paying the penalty for man's sins, thus reconciling man to God and delivering man from the executioner of God's righteous wrath against man's sin. (See pp. 217-240 in *The Blood of God* by Malcolm Webber.)

---

[203] *The sting of death is sin, and the power of sin is the law. (1 Cor. 15:56)*

[204] *Before this faith came, we were held prisoners by the law, locked up until faith should be revealed. (Gal. 3:23)*

[205] *For whoever keeps the whole law and yet stumbles at just one point is guilty of breaking all of it. (Jam. 2:10)*

[206] *by abolishing in his flesh the law with its commandments and regulations. His purpose was to create in himself one new man out of the two, thus making peace, (Eph. 2:15)*

[207] *Christ redeemed us from the curse of the law by becoming a curse for us, for it is written: "Cursed is everyone who is hung on a tree." (Gal. 3:13)*

Satan is not even the central focus of this verse (one of the principal rules of biblical interpretation requires us to always consider the verse's immediate context). It refers to all powers and authorities – good and bad. The good angels are also included here (v. 18) because it was through their ministry that the law was given (Deut. 33:2[208]; Acts 7:53[209]; Heb. 2:2[210]; Gal. 3:19[211]). Through Jesus' death on the cross, the law was abolished and thus the ministry of angels (who helped in the giving of the law) was put off, and they were revealed as subject to Him who is the sole Mediator between man and God and is the Head of every principality and power.

Paul's thrust, in the context of overall passage, is that Jesus is greater than all other realms of authority (including angelic, Eph. 1:21[212]; Phil. 2:9[213]) – therefore, don't get entangled with angelic mediators and religious pursuits other than Him. Paul's point is an exaltation of the Lord Jesus (cf. Heb. 1 & 2). He is pointing the Colossian believers to their completeness in the all-sufficient One.

> *disarmed.* Same verb as "putting off" in v. 11: the idea of getting out of one's clothes and then getting away from them. Not a military word. God has "stripped" the angelic authorities of whatever glory and eminence they formerly had.
>
> *he.* God the Father, not Christ. God is the subject throughout this passage (vv. 12-15).

---

[208] *He said: "The Lord came from Sinai and dawned over them from Seir; he shone forth from Mount Paran. He came with myriads of holy ones from the south, from his mountain slopes. (Deut. 33:2)*

[209] *you who have received the law that was put into effect through angels but have not obeyed it." (Acts 7:53)*

[210] *For if the message spoken by angels was binding, and every violation and disobedience received its just punishment, (Heb. 2:2)*

[211] *What, then, was the purpose of the law? It was added because of transgressions until the Seed to whom the promise referred had come. The law was put into effect through angels by a mediator. (Gal. 3:19)*

[212] *far above all rule and authority, power and dominion, and every title that can be given, not only in the present age but also in the one to come. (Eph. 1:21)*

[213] *Therefore God exalted him to the highest place and gave him the name that is above every name, (Phil. 2:9)*

***he made a public spectacle of them.*** Word is only used elsewhere in Matt. 1:19[214]. God displayed them as subordinate and subject to Jesus. No exhibition of them in disgrace is necessarily implied. The principalities and powers are exhibited in their true position of inferiority as mediators of an abolished law. Christ is revealed as the final and perfect manifestation of God.

***by the cross.*** Greek = "in it" or "in Him." The masculine and neuter pronouns have the same Greek form. Therefore, it could be translated "by the cross" (Jesus' cross was the instrument of triumph; this is the choice of many translators, and is consistent with v. 14) or "in Him" (referring to Jesus' triumphant exaltation). Certainly, this does not refer to any mythical triumph in hell!

### 2:16-23. SPECIFIC WARNINGS AGAINST THE FALSE TEACHINGS.

**16 Therefore do not let anyone judge you by what you eat or drink, or with regard to a religious festival, a New Moon celebration or a Sabbath day.**

***Therefore.*** Conclusion from the canceling of the law that was against us. This sheds further clarity on the meaning of v. 15. (If v. 15 were primarily about Jesus' defeat of Satan at the cross, how could Paul's words in v. 16ff possibly relate to it and follow logically from it?)

Since the law with all its ceremonies and rituals has been abolished, and since the angels have been shown to be subject to Christ (vv. 14-15), therefore don't follow teachings that bring you into bondage to ritual and asceticism, and promote the worship of angels (vv. 16-18). Those are all so much less than the Person of Jesus and they will only bring you into bondage.

You are complete in Christ. You have new life in Him. Let no one turn you to anything less!

***do not let anyone judge you.*** Don't allow anyone to sit in judgment on

---

[214] *Because Joseph her husband was a righteous man and did not want to expose her to public disgrace, he had in mind to divorce her quietly.* (Matt. 1:19)

you and to dictate what you must eat or drink (cf. Rom. 14:17[215]; 1 Cor. 8:8[216]; Heb. 9:10[217]; Mark 7:19[218]; 1 Tim. 4:1-5). The Christian life is a matter of inward life, not outward regulations.

**what you eat or drink.** The Mosaic law contained very few provisions concerning drinks (Lev. 10:9; 11:34, 36; Num. 6:3; Heb. 9:10), so it is probable that the false teachers had extended the prohibitions as to the use of wine by believers. Possibly, they also increased prohibitions regarding food – perhaps including all food from animals. Certainly, you may abstain from certain foods (e.g., fast food) for health reasons but not for religious reasons of holiness. Abstinence from certain foods may make you healthier but it will not make you holier.

**religious festival.** Greek = "holy day." The annual festivals or feast days (Lev. 23; e.g., Passover, Day of Atonement, Tabernacles).

***a New Moon celebration.*** The monthly festivals.

***a Sabbath day.*** The weekly observances. This same group of sacred days occurs elsewhere (e.g., 2 Chron. 2:4; 31:3; Ezek. 45:17; Hos. 2:11).

**17 *These are a shadow of the things that were to come; the reality, however, is found in Christ.***

This is why the believer should not continue in the observance of all the food laws and festivals of v. 16: in the Mosaic Law these things were only shadows or types of the reality who is Christ and who has now come in fullness.

**shadow.** Shadows are not realities; they merely possess a general resemblance to the reality (cf. Heb. 8:5[219]; 10:1[220]).

---

[215] *For the kingdom of God is not a matter of eating and drinking, but of righteousness, peace and joy in the Holy Spirit, (Rom. 14:17)*

[216] *But food does not bring us near to God; we are no worse if we do not eat, and no better if we do. (1 Cor. 8:8)*

[217] *They are only a matter of food and drink and various ceremonial washings – external regulations applying until the time of the new order. (Heb. 9:10)*

[218] *For it doesn't go into his heart but into his stomach, and then out of his body." (In saying this, Jesus declared all foods "clean.") (Mark 7:19)*

[219] *They serve at a sanctuary that is a copy and shadow of what is in heaven... (Heb. 8:5)*

[220] *The law is only a shadow of the good things that are coming – not the realities*

***the reality.*** Greek = "the body." The living body of which they were merely shadows: i.e., the substance, the reality. The Person of Jesus Christ is the reality: "Christ in you" (1:27).

You have the reality in Christ. You have the "better" covenant (Heb.). Why go back to shadows? These shadows include religious dietary ordinances and prohibitions as well as the observance of Sabbaths (whether on Saturday or Sunday) and holy days. We still need to rest – physically, mentally and emotionally – to be healthy (the spiritual principle contained in the original law, and affirmed by Jesus in Mark 6:31[221]), but that will not make us "holier" (Gal. 4:9-11).

**18 Do not let anyone who delights in false humility and the worship of angels disqualify you for the prize. Such a person goes into great detail about what he has seen, and his unspiritual mind puffs him up with idle notions.**

***who delights in false humility.*** The vain conceit of the teachers with their affectations of superior spirituality. In reality, they're full of spiritual pride.

***the worship of angels.*** Could be connected with false humility; they may have promoted the idea of worshipping angels since God is too holy and removed to be directly approached by man. Their assumption may have been that man, debased by contact with matter, must approach God through successive grades of intermediate beings. This verse gives us our only definite information that the false teachers worshipped angels (or at least had a very unhealthy obsession with them).

***disqualify you for the prize.*** Greek = "to act as a judge or umpire against you." To declare you unworthy of the prize. If you follow their teachings you will be robbed (1:23; 2:4, 8)!

***what he has seen.*** The false teachers were probably discussing in great detail their visions and revelations (not the Word of God) regarding lofty spiritual things. Some texts read, "what he has not seen." If so, Paul was referring to their actual ignorance in spite of their arrogant claims.

---

*themselves. For this reason it can never, by the same sacrifices repeated endlessly year after year, make perfect those who draw near to worship. (Heb. 10:1)*

[221] *Then, because so many people were coming and going that they did not even have a chance to eat, he said to them, "Come with me by yourselves to a quiet place and get some rest." (Mark 6:31)*

***his unspiritual mind.*** Greek = "the mind of his flesh." The teachers boasted of their higher spiritual truths; Paul describes their higher reason as fleshly and carnal.

***puffs him up.*** The emptiness of such pretension.

***idle notions.*** Paul's assessment of their "deeper truths."

**19 He has lost connection with the Head, from whom the whole body, supported and held together by its ligaments and sinews, grows as God causes it to grow.**

***He has lost connection with the Head.*** The false teacher has lost connection with Christ; that's how serious these errors are!

***the Head.*** Christ, as contrasted with the angelic mediators. Each believer must hold fast to the Head, and not only to other believers.

***from whom.*** Cf. Eph. 4:16.[222] The false teachers are separated from Christ and from His life.

***the whole body.*** In every one of its parts – not the body as a whole.

***its ligaments and sinews.*** The joints and bands of the body that bind together, and communicate between, limb and limb. Since the body grows together, Paul condemns the tendencies to spiritual exclusiveness. Each member must contribute to and share in the whole body's progress of growth. There are no spectators in Paul's vision for the church.; every member must grow, serve and build.

***grows.*** Present tense: the process is going on. It is inward, living connection with the Person of Christ that gives this growth – not the idle notions of esoteric religion.

**20 Since you died with Christ to the basic principles of this world, why, as though you still belonged to it, do you submit to its rules:**

***you died.*** Aorist tense indicates a definite event.

***with Christ.*** United with Him in His death, burial and resurrection (v. 11, ff; Rom. 6; Gal. 2:20; 6:14[223]).

---

[222] *From him the whole body, joined and held together by every supporting ligament, grows and builds itself up in love, as each part does its work. (Eph. 4:16)*

[223] *May I never boast except in the cross of our Lord Jesus Christ, through which the world has been crucified to me, and I to the world. (Gal. 6:14)*

***to the basic principles of this world.*** United with Christ, you died to sin, self, the law and the world. The basic principles or "rudiments" of this world include the rudimentary and carnal ritualistic approaches that they are now being influenced by: dietary regulations, ceremonial observances of feasts and holy days, etc. Cf. 2:8.

***why.*** Paul holds the Colossians responsible for their own spiritual direction. He does not merely blame the false teachers, but he also asks the believers, "Why are you listening to them?"

***as though you still belonged to it.*** You do not belong to this sphere of spiritual existence anymore. You died to it, and were raised alive to God.

***submit to its rules.*** Greek implies a sense of bondage. You died to legalism; why have you allowed yourselves to be brought into bondage by it again?

## 21 "Do not handle! Do not taste! Do not touch!"?

These are the rules that the false teachers are imposing on them in an effort to make them more holy. But the holiness is only outward. Purely outward religious observances have no effect on inward holiness. Paul is warning against asceticism. The asceticism could have involved avoidance of foods and drinks, certain unclean objects, even sexual relations.

## 22 These are all destined to perish with use, because they are based on human commands and teachings.

***These are all destined to perish with use.*** These words are probably a terse parenthesis.

***These.*** The foods and drinks, etc. that are forbidden.

***destined to perish.*** Greek = "are for corruption," in the physical sense of decomposition. The very use of these things destroys them (1 Cor. 6:13[224]); therefore, they are of no importance in the pursuit of holiness and spiritual maturity. If we destroy them by using them, they should not rule us.

***they are based on human commands and teachings.*** Refers to the precepts of v. 21.

***human.*** As contrasted with divine. The precepts are not only concerned with things that perish, but also have their source in human commandments.

---

[224] *"Food for the stomach and the stomach for food" – but God will destroy them both... (1 Cor. 6:13)*

***human commands and teachings.*** These are the "rudiments of the world" of v. 20. Cf. Matt. 15:1-20; Mark 7:1-23. They are not the realities of God, but only the commands and teachings of men.

Paul, like Jesus, condemns the human religious traditions as mere outward shows of holiness. (Both Paul and Jesus argue from the perishableness of meats and both treat these things as indifferent in themselves. Moreover, both condemn the human origin of the teachings.) True holiness is of the heart; the believer's heart has been changed through union with Christ and being made dead to sin and alive to God. Why, therefore, would believers wish to go back to useless observances of man? Ironically, this preoccupation with the flesh, although seeking to deny it, actually indulges its power over their lives.

In chapter 3, Paul will describe the spiritual and moral life of the believer in terms of character and relationships in the context of normal life – those are the elements of true spirituality, not self-centered ascetic laws and mystical religious practices.

***23 Such regulations indeed have an appearance of wisdom, with their self-imposed worship, their false humility and their harsh treatment of the body, but they lack any value in restraining sensual indulgence.***

***Such regulations.*** Paul refers to this broad class of teachings, not only to these individual ideas, but to this whole general approach to spirituality that they are following.

***self-imposed worship.*** Worship that is self-imposed or volunteered. The Greek carries the sense of pretense as well as the worship being self-chosen. It is only a self-chosen pretense of worship.

***false humility.*** It is merely the extravagant and ostentatious affectation of humility.

***harsh treatment.*** Greek refers to unsparing treatment or severity. Asceticism.

***but they lack any value.*** Paul contrasts the real value of these ascetic practices with their popular estimation. They have an appearance of spirituality; in reality, they have no value whatsoever.

***in restraining.*** Greek = "as a remedy against." These religious practices, while they appear to indicate superior wisdom and holiness, are, in reality, worthless against the flesh. It is only the inward life and power of the

Holy Spirit that is able to put the old man to death (Rom. 8:13[225]). Inward union with God is the true Christian life (John 17:3).

## 3:1 – 4:6. Second part of the epistle. Direct exhortations regarding the practical issues of the Christian life, founded on their union with the risen Christ.

As Paul often does in his letters, in Colossians he shares deep theological truth in the first half of the letter, and then he connects that theology to daily life in the second half of the letter.

In the first half of Colossians, Paul declares the theological preeminence and all-sufficiency of Jesus Christ. Jesus is God. He is above all. He is the Creator of all. Therefore, we should worship and serve Him only. We should not be led astray by false teachings that promote other objects of worship or that lower Christ's position. Moreover, Jesus Christ is all-sufficient. His death and resurrection delivered us from sin, Satan, self and the world. We need no other religious practice outside of union with Him to be saved or to go deeper in holiness and Christian maturity. Therefore, we reject all forms of external regulations and observances as paths to greater holiness. We reject all legalistic, ritualistic and ascetic approaches to holiness since the law was nailed to the cross – it was abolished in Jesus' death. Jesus is preeminent and all-sufficient. That was the central point of the first half of Colossians.

Now, Paul applies that preeminence and all-sufficiency to our daily lives. He takes the theological truths of chapters 1 and 2 and connects them to our daily lives, demonstrating that there is only one path to daily spiritual victory and maturity: union with Jesus Christ. There is only one path to holiness: union with Jesus (1:27; 2:10).

Paul thus sets forth the true path to holiness and spiritual maturity: union with Christ. Christ is preeminent and all-sufficient. We need no path to spiritual maturity and holiness other than union with Him. This daily union with Him will result in lives characterized by Christian virtues and relationships.

---

[225] *For if you live according to the sinful nature, you will die; but if by the Spirit you put to death the misdeeds of the body, you will live, (Rom 8:13)*

### 3:1-4. TRANSITION TO THE NEW SUBJECT AND THE GROUND OF THE COMING EXHORTATIONS.

*3:1 Since, then, you have been raised with Christ, set your hearts on things above, where Christ is seated at the right hand of God.*

- *you have been raised with Christ.* Progression from having died with Christ to this world (2:20). You have also been raised in union with Him to a new life (Rom. 6:4[226]).
- *set your hearts on things above.* In your daily lives, reckon yourselves to be dead to sin and alive to God (Rom. 6:11-13[227]; Matt. 6:33[228]). The practical consequences of the believer's union with Christ.
- *where Christ is seated at the right hand of God.* Cf. Eph. 2:6.[229] Since you are with Him your life will be involved in Him. This is a spiritual reality that should change your life.
- *at the right hand of God.* Our home with Christ is not merely in the heavenly places but is in the highest position there – at God's right hand!

This is how you achieve experiential holiness as a Christian: through daily union and communion with Christ. Paul sets forth the all-sufficiency of Christ with regard to the experiences of our daily lives and our pursuit of victory and maturity – it is all in Him!

*2 Set your minds on things above, not on earthly things.*

---

[226] *We were therefore buried with him through baptism into death in order that, just as Christ was raised from the dead through the glory of the Father, we too may live a new life. (Rom. 6:4)*

[227] *In the same way, count yourselves dead to sin but alive to God in Christ Jesus. Therefore do not let sin reign in your mortal body so that you obey its evil desires. Do not offer the parts of your body to sin, as instruments of wickedness, but rather offer yourselves to God, as those who have been brought from death to life; and offer the parts of your body to him as instruments of righteousness. (Rom 6:11-13)*

[228] *But seek first his kingdom and his righteousness, and all these things will be given to you as well. (Matt. 6:33)*

[229] *And God raised us up with Christ and seated us with him in the heavenly realms in Christ Jesus, (Eph. 2:6)*

***Set your minds.*** Establish your inward disposition – all of your thoughts, motives, desires, inward affection, devotion, etc. Let your life revolve around Him – your inward union with Him.

***on things above.*** Specifically on Him.

***earthly things.*** Sin, pride and worldliness, etc. (Phil. 3:19[230]), as well as the false religion Paul has been condemning (2:8, 18).

**3 For you died, and your life is now hidden with Christ in God.**

***For.*** Gives the reason for v. 2.

***you died.*** In union with Christ (2:20). Your old man, your past, your old struggles and weaknesses – they all died with Christ! The power of the past in your life in broken.

***your life is now hidden with Christ.*** You were raised in union with Christ. Therefore, your new spiritual life is no longer in the realm of the earthly and fleshly, but is with the life of the risen Lord Jesus (Phil. 3:20[231]), who is presently unseen (except by the eyes of faith) with God.

***hidden.*** Cf. 1 John 3:2.[232] Your life is so strongly united with Christ in God it is said to be "hidden" with Him.

***in God.*** Christ's own life is in God. Our union with God is in Him.

**4 When Christ, who is your life, appears, then you also will appear with him in glory.**

***who is your life.*** Your life is not only with Christ (v. 3); your life *is* Christ. This not only means that Jesus is the Possessor and Giver of eternal life; Jesus Christ Himself is the very essence, the very substance, of the Christian life. Jesus is personally, Himself, your life, and you possess life only by

---

[230] *Their destiny is destruction, their god is their stomach, and their glory is in their shame. Their mind is on earthly things. (Phil. 3:19)*

[231] *But our citizenship is in heaven. And we eagerly await a Savior from there, the Lord Jesus Christ, (Phil. 3:20)*

[232] *Dear friends, now we are children of God, and what we will be has not yet been made known. But we know that when he appears, we shall be like him, for we shall see him as he is. (1 John 3:2)*

union with Him and His resurrection. (Cf. John 14:6[233]; Phil. 1:21[234]; 1 John 5:11-12,[235] 20[236])

***appears.*** At his return (1 Cor. 1:7[237]; 2 Thess. 1:7[238]; 1 Pet. 1:7,[239] 13[240]; 4:13[241]).

***you also will appear with him in glory.*** Cf. John 17:20-24; 1 John 3:2[242]; Rom. 8:17.[243] We experience union with Christ now – inwardly, morally, spiritually, ethically. We shall possess the full and perfect manifestation (body, soul, mind and spirit) of our union with Him at His return.

This is the Christian's path to spiritual maturity – union with Christ in His death and resurrection. Just as there are no other mediators between man and God, and no supplemental truths other than the Person of Jesus Christ (Col. 1 – 2), so there is no path to inward peace, victory or freedom from sin and its effects (e.g., healing of the memories,

---

[233] *Jesus answered, "I am the way and the truth and the life. No one comes to the Father except through me." (John 14:6)*

[234] *For to me, to live is Christ... (Phil. 1:21)*

[235] *And this is the testimony: God has given us eternal life, and this life is in his Son. He who has the Son has life; he who does not have the Son of God does not have life. (1 John 5:11-12)*

[236] *...And we are in him who is true – even in his Son Jesus Christ. He is the true God and eternal life. (1 John 5:20)*

[237] *Therefore you do not lack any spiritual gift as you eagerly wait for our Lord Jesus Christ to be revealed. (1 Cor. 1:7)*

[238] *and give relief to you who are troubled, and to us as well. This will happen when the Lord Jesus is revealed from heaven in blazing fire with his powerful angels. (2 Thess. 1:7)*

[239] *These have come so that your faith – of greater worth than gold, which perishes even though refined by fire – may be proved genuine and may result in praise, glory and honor when Jesus Christ is revealed. (1 Pet. 1:7)*

[240] *Therefore, prepare your minds for action; be self-controlled; set your hope fully on the grace to be given you when Jesus Christ is revealed. (1 Pet. 1:13)*

[241] *But rejoice that you participate in the sufferings of Christ, so that you may be overjoyed when his glory is revealed. (1 Pet. 4:13)*

[242] *Dear friends, now we are children of God, and what we will be has not yet been made known. But we know that when he appears, we shall be like him, for we shall see him as he is. (1 John 3:2)*

[243] *Now if we are children, then we are heirs – heirs of God and co-heirs with Christ, if indeed we share in his sufferings in order that we may also share in his glory. (Rom. 8:17)*

psychological teachings and methods) other than union with Him. Other such paths may have the appearance of spirituality and look like "deeper truth" and deeper ways to deliverance and wholeness, but they are not biblical. What is biblical is the daily crucified life. That is your path to deliverance, wholeness in Christ, peace, victory and spiritual maturity. Popular contemporary teachers may promote supplemental practices, but since they are nowhere taught in the Scriptures and, in fact, an entirely different approach to deliverance and maturity is taught, we would be wise to avoid them. They will only confuse the believer and distract him from the real path of spiritual maturity. Just as external, legalistic regulations keep the believer living in the realm that is worldly and fleshly (2:20), so these practices keep the believer absorbed in the old man who, in reality, died with Christ.

Our path to victory is not to try to "fix" the old man (he can't be fixed; God put him to death!) or to focus on one's past life, or to "let all the hurts and pains out" (Prov. 29:11[244]), but it is to count the old man and the past life dead with Christ, and the new man alive to God – and to do that on a daily basis.

Our problem is that we want to find peace and emotional wholeness without going the path of death to self. That is why we embrace various supplemental paths.

You died with Christ, you were raised with Christ, your life is hid in Christ now, and your life will be revealed with Him in glory at His return – that is why you should live differently: because you are profoundly different! You are changed. You are free! You can do this. You are a new creation in Christ (2 Cor. 5:17[245]). Just as the law was nailed to the cross, so your old man was nailed to the cross, your past was nailed to the cross. You are free! But you must reckon this to be so on a daily basis. That daily reckoning is the method by which you will experience true freedom, true holiness and true spiritual maturity.

---

[244] *A fool gives full vent to his anger, but a wise man keeps himself under control. (Prov. 29:11)*

[245] *Therefore, if anyone is in Christ, he is a new creation; the old has gone, the new has come! (2 Cor. 5:17)*

There is no other "technique" or "method" of Christian victory offered in the New Testament. Jesus Christ is preeminent and all-sufficient.

Thus, the biblical process of inner victory consists of:

1. Genuine salvation through repentance and faith.
2. The inward filling of the Holy Spirit.
3. Deliverance from demonic oppression as necessary.
4. Being renewed by the Word of God.
5. Taking up our cross daily, deliberately counting ourselves to be dead to sin and the old man, and alive to God according to the new man in Christ. This means walking daily in fellowship with the Lord Jesus in continued faith and repentance. It includes developing the spiritual disciplines in our lives – prayer, forgiveness, Scripture study and meditation, fasting, resisting the devil, servanthood, accountability, taking responsibility for one's life, fellowship, praise, worship, giving, outreach, etc.

All the above principles of inner victory are taught and practiced in the New Testament. However, there are no techniques such as "healing of the memories" or other similar kinds of counseling taught anywhere in the Bible. Neither are they practiced anywhere. Jesus did not use such techniques; nor did Paul or anyone else. Those practices are simply not found in the New Testament – either in precept or example.

Such practices are based on misconceptions regarding the nature of man. Usually they propose that the inner soul of man is like a bucket or computer hard drive that somehow stores all the previous events of a person's life in such a way that they continue to determine his current inner state of mind and heart. Therefore, repressed memories must be individually uncovered (through a variety of means such as hypnosis, guided mental imagery, or dream interpretation) and confronted (again, through a variety of means such as visualizing Jesus going through the experience with you) and thereby "healed."

For example, one author wrote, "things we are unaware of need to be dealt with, whether physical or emotional. The subconscious mind is a reservoir – a holding tank – of memories, experiences, fears, traumas, and false beliefs… these things…need to be explored and healed."

In reality, memory is quite creative (making any attempt at bringing memories up to confront and "heal" them, perilous at best) and man's inner consciousness is dynamic, changing according to the decisions one makes on a continual basis. False memory syndrome has caused a multitude of problems in counseling situations even to the extreme of false accusations of satanic ritual abuse being made. Furthermore, rather than forgetting one's traumatic experiences, a much more common problem for people is that they cannot forget them!

Moreover, such conceptions promote a defeatist, deterministic approach to the believer's life – since one can never get totally free from one's past which inexorably determines one's present and future without one even being aware of it. Thus, these practices keep people in bondage to self, sin, and the past, and they encourage terminal self-absorption in those who are forever "recovering." One doesn't have time to serve in the church or win the lost, because one is too busy absorbed in self! Who has time for anything else?

Furthermore, if deliverance from past traumatic experiences requires that one directly and experientially confronts each trauma, then one needs to go back and re-live every sin one has ever committed since each sin is a highly traumatic experience (Jam. 2:10[246]). The biblical path to victory, in stark contrast, is concentration on Jesus Christ!

Paul says the believer has died to the old man, and has been raised with Christ to a new life in God. Those are not merely theories, but spiritual realities. As we reckon those to be so on a daily basis, we will experience them to be true. You are a new creation in Christ! Walk in it!

This is the biblical approach to peace and spiritual maturity. It is a simple approach: one doesn't need a doctorate in psychology to understand it. Anyone can understand it and live it, without being forever dependent upon the "experts" to help him find healing.

---

[246] *For whoever keeps the whole law and yet stumbles at just one point is guilty of breaking all of it. (Jam. 2:10)*

Some may argue that it is too simple an approach to daily victory. But how simple was it to get saved? You were bound by sin and the curse, doomed to eternal destruction, and merely by believing and receiving the truth of the gospel you were instantly and eternally saved! In the same way, if you will simply believe and receive the truth regarding your union with Jesus in His death and resurrection, you will be able to walk in victory! Reckon it to be so on a daily basis, and you will live in Christian victory.

Of course, while this path of death to self is relatively simple to grasp it is not necessarily easy to live! In fact, it is a daily battle (Gal. 5:17[247]); but we must be involved in the right battle, using the right weapons, and not distracted by other non-biblical pursuits.

Certainly, it is biblical for the believer to *reflect* on his life (present or past) before the Lord, asking the Holy Spirit to reveal areas of sin or unforgiveness that he is holding on to in his heart (Ps. 139:23-24[248]). Moreover, it may be beneficial to have another believer praying with him at this time for the full dealing of God with his heart. This, however, does not represent a seeking for "inner healing" or "healing of the memories" but rather repentance from the sin of bitterness or unforgiveness – this is not a healing of past events but repentance of present attitudes. Furthermore, this kind of prayer and "counseling" can be given by any believer in normal, healthy church life, not just by the "experts" who have to be specially "certified" in some technique.

Moreover, incorrect beliefs of and God and oneself do need to be addressed by the truth of God's Word. This does not take place through some therapeutical technique but rather through:

1. Revelation of Truth.
2. Conviction by the Holy Spirit.

---

[247] *For the sinful nature desires what is contrary to the Spirit, and the Spirit what is contrary to the sinful nature. They are in conflict with each other, so that you do not do what you want. (Gal. 5:17)*
[248] *Search me, O God, and know my heart; test me and know my anxious thoughts. See if there is any offensive way in me, and lead me in the way everlasting. (Ps. 139:23-24)*

3. Conversion – repentance and faith.
4. Walking daily in freedom, putting off the old man and putting on the new.

Additionally, the believer should be encouraged to express his true feelings to God regarding his disappointments with the past and his fears about the future, etc., as the psalmists and others did (e.g., Job, Ps. 22; Ps. 73; cf. 1 Sam. 1:10-20; Matt. 26:36-44; 2 Cor. 12:7-10). In this process, the believer, like the psalmists, will resolve his struggles and come to terms with the sovereign dealings of God in his own life. Again, this does not represent "healing of the memories" but a genuine submission and full surrender of the believer's heart to God and a deeper understanding of God's dealings.

The promoters of inner healing techniques do not usually tell the stories of those who have been hurt and confused by their methods. They do, however, have stories of apparent success. While we certainly rejoice with those who find greater freedom in Christ, we suspect that they find such freedom not through the inner healing techniques but rather through the biblical principles outlined above of union with Christ, forgiveness, submission to God, and so forth, which they encounter while in the midst of the techniques.

The Scriptures do not deal with everything in life; obviously, they don't mention cars or computers. But they do deal conclusively with spiritual life, emotional life and inner peace. This realm is their field. Consequently, while we do embrace and use the advances of science and technology, yet, when it comes to issues of inward life and spiritual life, the Bible truly is all we need. It is authoritative, comprehensive and conclusive.

## 3:5-17. PRACTICAL EXHORTATIONS TO WALK IN UNION WITH CHRIST – LAYING ASIDE THE OLD MAN (VV. 5-11) AND PUTTING ON THE NEW (VV. 12-17).

After summarizing the essence of our new life in Christ in vv. 1-4, Paul gives the details in vv. 5-17.

**5 Put to death, therefore, whatever belongs to your earthly nature: sexual immorality, impurity, lust, evil desires and greed, which is idolatry.**

*Put to death.* Aorist tense implies a single, decisive act. You are dead to sin, therefore you must live like it (Gal. 5:24[249]; Rom. 8:13[250]). You must daily live it out. Cf. the parallel passage in Eph. 4:17-32. God has already done this in Christ; you must do it daily in your life.

*therefore.* Because you died with Christ. In Christ you are dead to all these sins; therefore, live like it. You can!

*whatever belongs to your earthly nature.* Every kind of sin. Nothing need keep you in bondage; you are free! Jesus has given you absolute and complete victory.

Daily union with Christ is not merely one of many good paths to peace, spiritual wholeness and maturity. It is the *only* New Testament "method."

Paul's first list of sins relates primarily to human lust: sexual immorality and covetousness.

*sexual immorality.* Greek = "fornication." Sexual relations outside of marriage.
*impurity.* Natural sexual desires corrupted by sin.
*lust.* Improper sexual passion.
*greed.* Greek = "covetousness." In the context of lust. Has a climactic force: "and especially covetousness."
*which is idolatry.* Cf. Eph. 5:5.[251] Whatever you love and serve with your life is your god. The lust for wealth sets riches in the place of God.

**6 Because of these, the wrath of God is coming.**

---

[249] *Those who belong to Christ Jesus have crucified the sinful nature with its passions and desires. (Gal. 5:24)*

[250] *For if you live according to the sinful nature, you will die; but if by the Spirit you put to death the misdeeds of the body, you will live, (Rom. 8:13)*

[251] *For of this you can be sure: No immoral, impure or greedy person – such a man is an idolater – has any inheritance in the kingdom of Christ and of God. (Eph. 5:5)*

Cf. Eph. 5:6.[252] Man thinks these activities are all acceptable and sometimes even commendable (Rom. 1:32[253]), but God does not!

**the wrath of God.** His temporal and eternal wrath.

**7 You used to walk in these ways, in the life you once lived.**

**walk...lived.** "Walk" refers to their conduct and practices, "lived" to their condition (cf. Gal. 5:25[254]).
**once.** Before you were in Christ.

**8 But now you must rid yourselves of all such things as these: anger, rage, malice, slander, and filthy language from your lips.**

**But now.** Now that you no longer live in the old condition, your daily conduct must change (cf. Rom. 13:12[255]; Eph. 4:22,[256] 25[257]; Heb. 12:1[258]; Jam. 1:21[259]; 1 Pet. 2:1[260]).

---

[252] Let no one deceive you with empty words, for because of such things God's wrath comes on those who are disobedient. (Eph. 5:6)

[253] Although they know God's righteous decree that those who do such things deserve death, they not only continue to do these very things but also approve of those who practice them. (Rom. 1:32)

[254] If we live in the Spirit, let us also walk in the Spirit. (Gal. 5:25, NKJV)

[255] The night is nearly over; the day is almost here. So let us put aside the deeds of darkness and put on the armor of light. (Rom. 13:12)

[256] You were taught, with regard to your former way of life, to put off your old self, which is being corrupted by its deceitful desires; (Eph. 4:22)

[257] Therefore each of you must put off falsehood and speak truthfully to his neighbor, for we are all members of one body. (Eph. 4:25)

[258] Therefore, since we are surrounded by such a great cloud of witnesses, let us throw off everything that hinders and the sin that so easily entangles, and let us run with perseverance the race marked out for us. (Heb. 12:1)

[259] Therefore, get rid of all moral filth and the evil that is so prevalent and humbly accept the word planted in you, which can save you. (James 1:21)

[260] Therefore, rid yourselves of all malice and all deceit, hypocrisy, envy, and slander of every kind. (1 Pet. 2:1)

Being in Christ does not simply consist of making different ethical choices, but it is fundamentally a matter of living in a different condition. The different choices proceed from the different condition (and it can never be vice-versa).

***rid yourselves of all such things as these.*** It is your responsibility to do this. Moreover, you can do this – irrespective of your past! You are free! Believe it! Do it!

Paul's second list of sins concerns malignity in relationships.

***anger, rage, malice, slander, and filthy language.*** Cf. Eph. 4:31.[261]
***anger.*** Settled anger in the heart.
***rage.*** The sudden and passionate outburst of anger.
***malice.*** The feeling that prompts a man to hurt his neighbor in some way.
***slander.*** Libel, defame.
***filthy language.*** Greek = "foul-mouthed abuse."

**9 Do not lie to each other, since you have taken off your old self with its practices**

***Do not lie to each other.*** Cf. Eph. 4:25.[262]
***since.*** Righteous choices proceed from righteous inner life. The outward characteristics of the life of Christ proceed from the reality of the life of Christ dwelling in the believer.
***your old self.*** Cf. Rom. 6:6.[263]

Imagine wearing a coat with things such as sexual immorality, anger, rage, malice, etc. in its pockets. Then you take this coat off and discard it. The old life, and all its ways, are now gone!

Again, Paul stresses that the different condition of life precedes, and makes possible, the different choices in life. Thus, the outward characteristics of

---

[261] *Get rid of all bitterness, rage and anger, brawling and slander, along with every form of malice. (Eph. 4:31)*
[262] *Therefore each of you must put off falsehood and speak truthfully to his neighbor, for we are all members of one body. (Eph. 4:25)*
[263] *For we know that our old self was crucified with him so that the body of sin might be done away with, that we should no longer be slaves to sin – (Rom. 6:6)*

new life are not externally imposed but internally generated from union with Christ.

**10 and have put on the new self, which is being renewed in knowledge in the image of its Creator.**

- **and have put on the new self.** You have put off the old "coat" (life) and have put on the new one.
- **being renewed.** Present participle: in process of continuous renewal (2 Cor. 4:16[264]). You are in the Kingdom of Light (1:13), but you must engage in the process of spiritual maturity. New believers are babes in Christ who must grow.
- **in knowledge.** Greek = "unto perfect knowledge": the end to which the renewal is heading (Eph. 4:13[265]). This knowledge excludes all the vices just mentioned.
- **in the image of its Creator.** Greek = "after the image of its Creator." Cf. Eph. 4:24.[266]
- **its Creator.** God.

**11 Here there is no Greek or Jew, circumcised or uncircumcised, barbarian, Scythian, slave or free, but Christ is all, and is in all.**

All those just-mentioned sins are inconsistent with the believer's new life in Christ, which has abolished even the deep distinctions that have divided humanity into hostile camps. Verses 8-9 dealt with sins involving one-on-one relationships. Verse 11 deals with corporate relational divisions.

- **Here.** In the new life in Christ.
- **there is no.** Very strong in the Greek. Signifies not merely the fact, but the impossibility: there is no room for.

---

[264] *Therefore we do not lose heart. Though outwardly we are wasting away, yet inwardly we are being renewed day by day.* (2 Cor. 4:16)

[265] *until we all reach unity in the faith and in the knowledge of the Son of God and become mature, attaining to the whole measure of the fullness of Christ.* (Eph. 4:13)

[266] *and to put on the new self, created to be like God in true righteousness and holiness.* (Eph. 4:24)

Paul specifies national, religious, cultural and social diversities (Gal. 3:28[267] adds the gender distinctive) and disallows them all in Christ. Every distinctive category of humanity is done away as to worth or privilege. We still are men and women, slaves and free, etc., and we have all the attendant responsibilities of those roles, but there are no divisions in Christ.

***Christ is all, and is in all.*** We are one with Christ; therefore, we are one with each other in Him. In Christ, we have unity.

This is why we must not follow the popular idea of "putting aside our differences" to work together with those of other religions to seek a "higher goal" such as racial reconciliation or justice for the poor. Jesus is preeminent. He is our goal. Moreover, in Him we find true and eternally lasting racial reconciliation and justice for the poor, etc.!

**3:12-17. PRACTICAL EXHORTATIONS TO PUT ON THE NEW MAN.**

Paul progresses from putting the old self off to putting the new man on.

***12 Therefore, as God's chosen people, holy and dearly loved, clothe yourselves with compassion, kindness, humility, gentleness and patience.***

***Therefore.*** You have put on the new man in Christ (v. 10), and you are one in Him (v. 11), so live like it.
***God's chosen people.*** Greek = "elect of God." God chose you before creation (Eph. 1:4[268]; 1 Thess. 1:4[269]; Rom. 8:33[270]; Tit. 1:1[271]). Live like God's elect. Live according to the extraordinary destiny God has given you!
***holy and dearly loved.*** Both are due to His choosing.

---

[267] *There is neither Jew nor Greek, slave nor free, male nor female, for you are all one in Christ Jesus. (Gal. 3:28)*
[268] *For he chose us in him before the creation of the world to be holy and blameless in his sight… (Eph. 1:4)*
[269] *knowing, beloved brethren, your election by God. (1 Thess. 1:4, NKJV)*
[270] *Who shall bring a charge against God's elect? It is God who justifies. (Rom. 8:33, NKJV)*
[271] *Paul, a bondservant of God and an apostle of Jesus Christ, according to the faith of God's elect and the acknowledgment of the truth which accords with godliness, (Titus 1:1, NKJV)*

***dearly loved.*** By God. You are dearly loved by Him.
***compassion, kindness, humility, gentleness and patience.*** Primarily toward each other, in this context (Eph. 4:2[272]).

Now you put on a new coat with things such as compassion, kindness, humility, etc. in its pockets. Your life is now different! Therefore, reckon it to be so in your daily life.

This is how you "clothe" yourself with His life and character. This is the daily life process of walking in the Spirit, and growing as a Christian. In every temptation to sin, look inside to the life of Christ in you (1:27). As you look to Him, He will help you bear the fruit of the Spirit; He will be your new life. There are three steps to this: first, believe that God has crucified the old man with Christ and made you new – alive to God in Christ. Second, look inside for the new life that is in you. Third, yield to it, instead of the flesh. There will be a battle between the flesh and the Spirit (Gal. 5:17), but you are able now to choose the Spirit. At first it is easier to follow the flesh due to the habits of life you have, but as you choose the Spirit, more and more that will become easier and more natural. This is the process of Christian maturity.

**13 Bear with each other and forgive whatever grievances you may have against one another. Forgive as the Lord forgave you.**

***Bear with each other.*** Be patient.
***forgive...one another.*** Greek = "forgive yourselves." Emphasizes the fact that they are all members of Christ's body, so, in forgiving each other they forgive themselves. Cf. Gal. 5:15.[273]
***Whatever.*** Whether they are "justified" or not.
***grievances.*** Greek = "cause of blame."
***Forgive as the Lord forgave you.*** Do for each other, what God did once for you all (Eph. 4:32[274]). This is not an option. What He forgave you was

---

[272] *Be completely humble and gentle; be patient, bearing with one another in love. (Eph. 4:2)*
[273] *If you keep on biting and devouring each other, watch out or you will be destroyed by each other. (Gal. 5:15)*
[274] *Be kind and compassionate to one another, forgiving each other, just as in Christ God forgave you. (Eph. 4:32)*

infinite; what you forgive each other is very small in comparison (Matt. 18:21-35).

This is what the mature believer looks like. Christian maturity does not consist of endless visions and flakes of gold dust, but of the character qualities of Christ expressed in your life.

**14 And over all these virtues put on love, which binds them all together in perfect unity.**

*over all.* Put on, like an upper garment.

*love.* Greek = "the love." The well-known love that is fitting for Christians. This is not sentimental or romantic love, but divine love.

*which binds them all together in perfect unity.* Love embraces, completes and binds together all the rest, which, without it, are all scattered virtues. Love binds the virtues together, and will bind the believers together too. When the overarching power of love binds the believers together, perfect unity is achieved.

Paul is describing the corporate life of the new man in Christ. This comes from the overflowing reality of individual new life. We can have this in our churches!

This love that unifies is not a human love, but the life of Christ within His people and so it is totally consistent with holiness of life, true doctrine, etc., all of which are usually seen as "unloving" and therefore divisive. Thus, Christian unity comes from indwelling divine life, which is the basis of Christian unity (John 17:21-22[275]), and not from human efforts to achieve "unity" through ignoring doctrine or compromising holiness.

**15 Let the peace of Christ rule in your hearts, since as members of one body you were called to peace. And be thankful.**

---

[275] *that all of them may be one, Father, just as you are in me and I am in you. May they also be in us so that the world may believe that you have sent me. I have given them the glory that you gave me, that they may be one as we are one: (John 17:21-22)*

***the peace of Christ.*** The peace that comes from Christ (John 14:27[276]).

***rule.*** Greek = "be umpire." Let the peace of Christ decide. In the context of daily life, in any course of action, choose that which will maintain peace among the brethren.

***as members of one body you were called to peace.*** Avoid anything that would bring disunity since you are members of one body. (Cf. Eph. 4:1-6.)

***thankful.*** To God who called you (Eph. 5:4[277]).

This verse taken on its own is frequently used to show how to receive guidance from God for personal decisions (i.e., let the peace of God in your heart determine which way you should go), but it does not refer to that. It refers to peace and unity in the body of Christ.

**16 Let the word of Christ dwell in you richly as you teach and admonish one another with all wisdom, and as you sing psalms, hymns and spiritual songs with gratitude in your hearts to God.**

Therefore a passion for the Word of God does not stand in contradiction to unity (v. 14) or peace (v. 15). In this context, the rich indwelling of God's Word is directly related to spiritual maturity and daily Christian victory.

***the word of Christ.*** The word spoken by Christ. The only occurrence of this phrase in the New Testament.

***richly.*** In abundance and fullness. The rich indwelling in you of the Word of Christ will result in its rich outflowing from you in words of teaching and admonishment as well as songs of praise.

***teach and admonish one another with all wisdom.*** Cf. 1:28. Here, not only the leaders and teachers are to do it, but every member should participate in this, ministering encouragement and life to each other in the context of daily life and interaction.

***admonish.*** This is not a contradiction to v. 15. "Unity" and "peace" do not preclude correcting or dealing with issues.

---

[276] *Peace I leave with you; my peace I give you. I do not give to you as the world gives. Do not let your hearts be troubled and do not be afraid. (John 14:27)*

[277] *Nor should there be obscenity, foolish talk or coarse joking, which are out of place, but rather thanksgiving. (Eph 5:4)*

***one another.*** Greek = "yourselves." Again (v. 13), as members one of another, when they teach each other they are teaching themselves.
***as you sing psalms, hymns and spiritual songs.*** Cf. Eph. 5:19.[278]
***psalms.*** An Old Testament psalm or a composition having that character.
***hymns.*** A song of praise.
***spiritual songs.*** Possibly spontaneous songs, given by the Holy Spirit, out of the richness of the Word of Christ in their hearts.

**17 And whatever you do, whether in word or deed, do it all in the name of the Lord Jesus, giving thanks to God the Father through him.**

General exhortation, summing up all the preceding ones.

***do it all in the name of the Lord Jesus.*** Not a reference to a formal invocation of His name. Do everything in union and fellowship with Him (cf. Eph. 5:20[279]). In every word and action, live in His presence, in obedience to Him, with the conviction of His approval and for the sake of His honor and glory. Live in constant fellowship with Him, in continual awareness of His presence and purpose.

### 3:18 – 4:1. VARIOUS EXHORTATIONS REGARDING SPECIFIC SOCIAL DUTIES.
#### 3:18-19. TO THE MARRIED.
#### 3:20-21. TO CHILDREN AND PARENTS.
#### 3:22–4:1. TO SLAVES AND MASTERS.

Cf. Eph. 5:22 – 6:9; 1 Pet. 2:18 – 3:7; Tit. 2:1-5.

Christian life is properly motivated by the mindfulness of the "things above," where our lives are hid with Christ in God (3:1-3). Thus, the holiness and values of that life will pervade all other aspects of life. There are not two modes of conduct – the spiritual and the secular. We should always live

---

[278] *Speak to one another with psalms, hymns and spiritual songs. Sing and make music in your heart to the Lord, (Eph. 5:19)*
[279] *always giving thanks to God the Father for everything, in the name of our Lord Jesus Christ. (Eph. 5:20)*

according to the new man. In fact, those who are genuinely saved will have had their home and work lives transformed by His grace. True spirituality will be demonstrated in the home and workplace.

Even though we are all one in Christ (3:11), yet the human distinctions have not been done away with. All of us still have many obligations regarding various social responsibilities. Christianity does not undermine the normal institutions of society. It does transform and recast them (since ultimately, we are serving God and not man), but in doing so, actually strengthens them.

**18 Wives, submit to your husbands, as is fitting in the Lord.**

*as is fitting.* The sense of obligation or duty. This is appropriate for the truly spiritual woman.
*in the Lord.* The realm of the duty: in the Lord. Because you're in Christ you have this obligation.

**19 Husbands, love your wives and do not be harsh with them.**

This verse is greatly expanded in Eph. 5:25-33. There is no rod of iron in the clenched hand of this man, to whom his wife submits, but only nails in the open hands of the one who is submitting himself to the death of the cross on behalf of his wife.

*do not be harsh.* Greek = "be not embittered." Do not be harsh or irritable.

This is the truly spiritual man. The mark of true spirituality is not how many verses you can quote, or how many hours each day you pray, but how you treat your wife!

**20 Children, obey your parents in everything, for this pleases the Lord.**

*obey your parents in everything.* Cf. Eph. 6:1.[280]
*in everything.* Except when it would constitute sin.

---

[280] *Children, obey your parents in the Lord, for this is right. (Eph. 6:1)*

***this pleases the Lord.*** The consequences of this are outlined in Eph. 6:2-3.[281]
If you want to please God, here's how to do it.

**21 Fathers, do not embitter your children, or they will become discouraged.**

Leadership principle: Leaders must be careful not to do this with their spiritual "children" as well.

***Fathers.*** Paul does not address mothers; it is not as necessary to do so.
***embitter.*** Greek = "provoke to anger." Cf. Eph. 6:4.[282]
***discouraged.*** They will lose heart. Possibly, Paul's meaning is that if the fathers continually irritate their children by exacting demands and perpetual fault-finding and interference for interference's sake, it will cause repeated punishment, and eventual discouragement on the child's part. His spirit will be broken and since what he does leads to constant failure and blame, he will lose hope of ever being able to succeed or to please. He may give obedience but it will be soulless.

Too many fathers speak negatively and harshly to their children. We must speak life to our children. Moreover, we must also express our love to them – verbally and with physical contact. We should not just do things for them and expect them to "get the message" that we love them! (Or else we should not be surprised when our children end up in street gangs or religious cults, searching for the love, acceptance and identification that we have not given them.)

Punishment sometimes requires physical expression; so does love. From the time of their birth, our children should be constantly touched, held, kissed, hugged, cuddled and verbally affirmed.

A story from David Morken: When our eldest son, Hubert, was a little fellow we were visiting at Balboa in southern California. One day we went out to look at the beautiful ships in the harbor, and Hubert seemed to want every one

---

[281] *"Honor your father and mother" – which is the first commandment with a promise – "that it may go well with you and that you may enjoy long life on the earth." (Eph. 6:2-3)*
[282] *And you, fathers, do not provoke your children to wrath, but bring them up in the training and admonition of the Lord. (Eph. 6:4)*

of them. He would say with boyish excitement, "Oh, Daddy, wouldn't you like to have that one?" And he would point his chubby finger at a gleaming motor cruiser, or a sleek sailboat. As we approached a bigger more luxurious vessel that cost (so we learned) about $800,000, again Hubert said, "Daddy, wouldn't you like to have that one?" "Hubert", I replied, "let me ask you a question. Suppose a man were to come to Daddy and say, 'Mr. Morken, I want to give you a choice between two things. You may become owner of all these ships in the harbor, and we will add to them the Queen Mary, the Queen Elizabeth, and all the ships of the president lines. (Hubert was interested in ocean liners!) Furthermore, I will give you enough money to operate them all. That's the first choice. Or (and I pointed to Hubert) you may have this little boy.' Now which do you think Daddy would choose?" Without a moment's hesitancy my son replied "Why, Daddy, I think you'd choose me."

With all he could have said about the duties of fathers, Paul focuses on this one issue of fathering, demonstrating its relative importance.

Paul now addresses slaves and masters.

***22 Slaves, obey your earthly masters in everything; and do it, not only when their eye is on you and to win their favor, but with sincerity of heart and reverence for the Lord.***

- ***obey.*** Paul does not counsel them here to try to win their freedom (cf. 1 Cor. 7:20-24). Similarly, leaders in today's suffering church around the world rarely ask for prayer for escape from suffering, but for strength to endure.
- ***earthly masters.*** Emphasizes that God is their real heavenly Master, although temporarily, you do have earthly masters to whom you must submit.
- ***in everything.*** Very simple instruction! Naturally, this does not include breaking the law.
- ***when their eye is on you.*** Greek = "with eye-service." (This word may have been coined by Paul.) Cf. Eph. 6:6.[283] Service that is most zealous when the eye of the master is upon them.

---

[283] *not with eyeservice, as men-pleasers, but as bondservants of Christ, doing the will of God from the heart, (Eph .6:6, NKJV)*

*sincerity.* Greek = "singleness": without duplicity. "Eye-service" is duplicity: you serve them faithfully when they're watching you and not so well at other times.

*for the Lord.* Cf. Eph. 6:5.[284] He is your true master who you serve at all times and in all you do. Moreover, if you're serving God, you can only do this by conscientious performance of your responsibilities quite apart from any recognition you receive from men. It doesn't matter whether they see you and give you favor (a raise or promotion) or not.

**23 Whatever you do, work at it with all your heart, as working for the Lord, not for men,**

Cf. Eph. 6:7[285]

*Whatever you do.* Every aspect of your life and service. There is no distinction here between secular and spiritual work.

*not for men.* Is an absolute. The idea of doing things "for men" is to be laid aside altogether. You are not serving "man and God"; in reality, you are exclusively serving the Lord.

**24 since you know that you will receive an inheritance from the Lord as a reward. It is the Lord Christ you are serving.**

*since you know.* Your grounds for sincere service.

*an inheritance…as a reward.* The inheritance is the reward (Eph. 6:8[286]).

*from the Lord.* Your reward will come from Him, so serve Him now. Moreover, this stands in marked contrast to their present condition as slaves who receive little compensation!

*It is the Lord Christ you are serving.* Ultimately you are not serving men at all but the Lord.

---

[284] *Slaves, obey your earthly masters with respect and fear, and with sincerity of heart, just as you would obey Christ. (Eph. 6:5)*

[285] *Serve wholeheartedly, as if you were serving the Lord, not men, (Eph. 6:7)*

[286] *because you know that the Lord will reward everyone for whatever good he does, whether he is slave or free. (Eph. 6:8)*

**25 Anyone who does wrong will be repaid for his wrong, and there is no favoritism.**

**repaid for his wrong.** There is not only reward for righteousness, but also "repayment" for wrongs.
**Anyone who does wrong.** Applies to all (cf. Eph. 6:8).
**there is no favoritism.** Master as well as slave will be punished for doing wrong. At the Last Day, everyone, without regard to position or wealth, shall receive his right judgment.

This verse may be directed to the slaves by way of encouragement to them to regard Jesus as their Lord and Master and to serve Him, seeing that all the many wrongs that happen to them in this life will be righted in the end if they leave them in His hands. This is also an encouragement to them not to do wrong themselves – they should not presume on their Christianity or on their slavehood (cf. 1 Tim. 6:1-2[287]).

**4:1 Masters, provide your slaves with what is right and fair, because you know that you also have a Master in heaven.**

**provide.** The Greek implies "on your part." Paul's counsel to Christian slave-owners is not that they set the slaves free. Social change is not God's agenda. Heart change is His concern. Serving and glorifying God in whatever circumstances we are is His agenda.
**fair.** Greek = "the equality." Not equality of material condition as in literal emancipation, but the deeper brotherly equality that grows out of the Christian relation in which there is neither bond nor free (Philemon 16[288]). Do not exploit or abuse them.
**you also have a Master.** As you are masters to them, so the Lord is to you.

---

[287] *All who are under the yoke of slavery should consider their masters worthy of full respect, so that God's name and our teaching may not be slandered. Those who have believing masters are not to show less respect for them because they are brothers. Instead, they are to serve them even better, because those who benefit from their service are believers, and dear to them. These are the things you are to teach and urge on them. (1 Tim. 6:1-2)*

[288] *no longer as a slave, but better than a slave, as a dear brother. He is very dear to me but even dearer to you, both as a man and as a brother in the Lord. (Philemon 16)*

### 4:2-6. CONCLUDING GENERAL EXHORTATIONS.
#### 4:2-4. EXHORTATIONS TO PRAYER.
#### 4:5-6. EXHORTATIONS REGARDING THEIR BEHAVIOR IN THE WORLD.

*2 Devote yourselves to prayer, being watchful and thankful.*

**Devote yourselves to prayer.** Greek = "continue steadfastly in prayer." Cf. Acts 2:42[289]; 6:4[290]; Rom. 12:12[291]; 1 Thess. 5:17.[292]

**prayer.** For themselves and for Paul also (v. 3).

**being watchful.** Being vigilant and alert in your prayer (1 Pet. 5:8[293]; Eph. 6:18[294]).

**and thankful.** This characterizes the watchfulness. Because you are thankful for the graces of God, you will watch over them in prayer to protect against losing them.

Prayer should be continuous, watchful and thankful.

*3 And pray for us, too, that God may open a door for our message, so that we may proclaim the mystery of Christ, for which I am in chains.*

**us.** For Paul's fellow-workers too. Paul does not solicit prayer for his personal welfare or financial prosperity, but always for the furtherance of the Gospel.

---

[289] *And they continued steadfastly in the apostles' doctrine and fellowship, in the breaking of bread, and in prayers. (Acts 2:42, NKJV)*

[290] *"but we will give ourselves continually to prayer and to the ministry of the word." (Acts 6:4)*

[291] *rejoicing in hope, patient in tribulation, continuing steadfastly in prayer; (Rom. 12:12, NKJV)*

[292] *pray continually; (1 Thess. 5:17)*

[293] *Be self-controlled and alert. Your enemy the devil prowls around like a roaring lion looking for someone to devour. (1 Pet. 5:8)*

[294] *And pray in the Spirit on all occasions with all kinds of prayers and requests. With this in mind, be alert and always keep on praying for all the saints. (Eph. 6:18)*

***a door for our message.*** Cf. Eph. 6:19[295]; 1 Cor. 16:9[296]; 2 Cor. 2:12[297]; Rev. 3:8.[298] Possibly a reference to his release from imprisonment (Philemon 2[299]). Certainly, Paul refers to the opening of opportunity for the extension of the gospel around the world.

***for which I am in chains.*** Paul is now a prisoner on account of his bold proclamation of the gospel.

***4 Pray that I may proclaim it clearly, as I should.***

***clearly.*** And boldly (Eph. 6:20[300]) in the face of the adversaries (1 Cor. 16:9[301]).

Paul requested prayer so it is most certainly not a lack of faith to request prayer for one's own ministry.

### 4:5-6. EXHORTATIONS REGARDING THEIR BEHAVIOR IN THE WORLD.

These are continued expressions of the life of the new man in the context of daily life.

***5 Be wise in the way you act toward outsiders; make the most of every opportunity.***

---

[295] *Pray also for me, that whenever I open my mouth, words may be given me so that I will fearlessly make known the mystery of the gospel,* (Eph. 6:19)

[296] *because a great door for effective work has opened to me, and there are many who oppose me.* (1 Cor. 16:9)

[297] *Now when I went to Troas to preach the gospel of Christ and found that the Lord had opened a door for me,* (2 Cor. 2:12)

[298] *I know your deeds. See, I have placed before you an open door that no one can shut. I know that you have little strength, yet you have kept my word and have not denied my name.* (Rev. 3:8)

[299] *And one thing more: Prepare a guest room for me, because I hope to be restored to you in answer to your prayers.* (Philemon 22)

[300] *for which I am an ambassador in chains. Pray that I may declare it fearlessly, as I should.* (Eph. 6:20)

[301] *because a great door for effective work has opened to me, and there are many who oppose me.* (1 Cor. 16:9)

***Be wise in the way you act toward outsiders.*** Cf. Eph. 5:15[302]; Matt. 10:16.[303]
**outsiders.** Non-Christians. Many non-Christians justify their unbelief by pointing to the hypocrisy of believers. Believers represent Christ and authenticate His salvation by our lives and words.
**make the most of every opportunity.** Greek = "redeeming the time." Buy up every favorable opportunity. Cf. Eph. 5:16.[304] Exactly what you have opportunity for will vary between circumstances, but always look for the cause of Christ to be advanced in some way in every situation. "Preach the gospel at all times. Use words if necessary." (St. Francis of Assisi)

1 Peter 3:15[305] gives an example of one way for this to happen. We should minister the gospel "with gentleness and respect" in contrast to the traditional antagonistic, aggressive, "in your face" style of evangelism.

***6 Let your conversation be always full of grace, seasoned with salt, so that you may know how to answer everyone.***

**conversation.** Words, speech.
**grace.** Gracious and winning favor. Sweet and courteous.
**seasoned.** Greek = "prepared."
**seasoned with salt.** Salt is used to make food more palatable. (By both Greek and Latin authors, the idea of salt was used to express the spiciness and wittiness of speech.) Cf. Eph. 4:29.[306] Not speech that is insipid and weak, or foolish, or corrupt, or prattling on and on. Speech that is wise, clear, vital, purposeful and meaningful. This does not forbid appropriate humor but it should not be "nonsense for its own sake" – it should be witty and purposeful.

---

[302] *Be very careful, then, how you live – not as unwise but as wise, (Eph. 5:15)*

[303] *I am sending you out like sheep among wolves. Therefore be as shrewd as snakes and as innocent as doves. (Matt 10:16)*

[304] *making the most of every opportunity, because the days are evil. (Eph. 5:16)*

[305] *But in your hearts set apart Christ as Lord. Always be prepared to give an answer to everyone who asks you to give the reason for the hope that you have. But do this with gentleness and respect, (1 Pet. 3:15)*

[306] *Do not let any unwholesome talk come out of your mouths, but only what is helpful for building others up according to their needs, that it may benefit those who listen. (Eph. 4:29)*

*so that you may know how to answer everyone.* So you may speak appropriately to each individual, with his particular needs, with whom you may come in contact.

### 4:7-18. PAUL CLOSES THE EPISTLE.
#### 4:7-9. COMMENDATION OF THE BEARERS OF THE EPISTLE: TYCHICUS AND ONESIMUS.
#### 4:10-14. VARIOUS GREETINGS FROM BRETHREN.
#### 4:15-17. VARIOUS GREETINGS TO FRIENDS.
#### 4:18. PAUL'S PERSONAL GREETING.

*7 Tychicus will tell you all the news about me. He is a dear brother, a faithful minister and fellow servant in the Lord.*

**Tychicus.** Is mentioned in Acts 20:4; Eph. 6:21; 2 Tim. 4:12; Tit. 3:12. He was sent at this time with this letter and also with the letter to the Ephesians.
***a dear brother.*** Dear to Paul.
***minister.*** Possibly to Paul himself (cf. Acts 19:22; 20:4).
***servant.*** Of Jesus Christ.

*8 I am sending him to you for the express purpose that you may know about our circumstances and that he may encourage your hearts.*

Cf. Eph. 6:21.[307]

***our circumstances.*** Paul wants to relieve their anxiety regarding his condition at Rome.

*9 He is coming with Onesimus, our faithful and dear brother, who is one of you. They will tell you everything that is happening here.*

**Onesimus.** Philemon 10[308]. Philemon's runaway slave who was rescued and

---

[307] *Tychicus, the dear brother and faithful servant in the Lord, will tell you everything, so that you also may know how I am and what I am doing.* (Eph. 6:21)
[308] *I appeal to you for my son Onesimus, who became my son while I was in chains.* (Philemon 10)

converted by Paul and then sent back to his master, with the letter to Philemon sent at the same time as this letter.

***our faithful and dear brother.*** The Colossians had known him only as a worthless, runaway slave (Philemon 11,[309] 16[310]). Paul speaks of him so affectionately to help him find a welcome reception at his home.

***one of you.*** Probably a native of your town. Philemon was probably also of Colosse.

***everything that is happening here.*** At Rome.

### 4:10-14. VARIOUS GREETINGS FROM BRETHREN.

***10 My fellow prisoner Aristarchus sends you his greetings, as does Mark, the cousin of Barnabas. (You have received instructions about him; if he comes to you, welcome him.)***

***Aristarchus.*** Mentioned in Acts 19:29; 20:4; 27:2; Philemon 24.

***Mark, the cousin of Barnabas.*** This may be why Barnabas took a more favorable view of Mark's defection than Paul (Acts 15:37-39). Barnabas knew Mark better so he took a different view of his behavior. However, Paul was justified in being cautious. So, who was right in their disagreement? The answer is that they both had good reasons for their different convictions regarding Mark. In Acts 15 they found a very positive outcome after the initial "sharp disagreement" (Acts 15:39): they agreed to disagree, with the help of the brothers at Antioch (Acts 15:40), and no doubt blessed one another as they went their separate ways. They did not have a "big extended fight" and depart from each other "in a huff," as is so often suggested, but gave us an excellent model of successful conflict resolution.

***instructions.*** We don't know what these were, but they were, no doubt, positive instructions ("welcome him").

---

[309] *Formerly he was useless to you, but now he has become useful both to you and to me. (Philemon 11)*

[310] *no longer as a slave, but better than a slave, as a dear brother. He is very dear to me but even dearer to you, both as a man and as a brother in the Lord. (Philemon 16)*

**11 Jesus, who is called Justus, also sends greetings. These are the only Jews among my fellow workers for the kingdom of God, and they have proved a comfort to me.**

**Jesus, who is called Justus.** The only one here who is not mentioned in Philemon. He is entirely unknown elsewhere in the Scripture.
**the only Jews among my fellow workers.** The Judaistic teachers, who should have been the most zealous for the Kingdom, were generally in opposition to Paul.
**comfort.** Encouragement.

**12 Epaphras, who is one of you and a servant of Christ Jesus, sends greetings. He is always wrestling in prayer for you, that you may stand firm in all the will of God, mature and fully assured.**

**Epaphras.** The one who probably planted this church is travailing in prayer for her maturity.
**wrestling in prayer.** Greek = "agonizing, wrestling, striving, struggling." Cf. 1:29–2:1; Rom. 15:30[311]; Is. 62:6-7.[312]
**in all the will of God.** In everything that God wills.
**mature.** Cf. 1:28.
**fully assured.** Cf. 2:2. Firm in the faith, resisting errors.

**13 I vouch for him that he is working hard for you and for those at Laodicea and Hierapolis.**

**working hard.** Greek word means hard labor to the point of pain. The word is often used of the toil of conflict in war. Description of his intense travailing prayer.
**Laodicea and Hierapolis.** Cities in the same region. Epaphras may have planted all three churches, and they may all have been under attack from

---

[311] *I urge you, brothers, by our Lord Jesus Christ and by the love of the Spirit, to join me in my struggle by praying to God for me. (Rom. 15:30)*
[312] *I have posted watchmen on your walls, O Jerusalem; they will never be silent day or night. You who call on the Lord, give yourselves no rest, and give him no rest till he establishes Jerusalem and makes her the praise of the earth. (Is. 62:6-7)*

the false teachings. In New Testament times, churches in the same region worked together closely. The New Testament picture was: one church in a city or town (1 Cor. 1:2[313]), made up of smaller groups of believers who meet in homes (1 Cor. 16:19[314]); and one group of churches in a region or country (1 Cor. 16:19[315]) with a corporate regional identity (see *Church Planting in the Book of Acts* by Malcolm Webber for more on this).

**14 Our dear friend Luke, the doctor, and Demas send greetings.**

- ***Our dear friend Luke, the doctor.*** Greek = "Luke the physician, the beloved." The fact that Luke was a doctor appears in his writings: he uses common technical medical words and phrases in his descriptions of diseases or of miracles of healing.
- ***Demas.*** Mentioned in Philemon 24; 2 Tim. 4:10.[316] The absence of any honorable or endearing mention here may be due to the commencement of Demas' apostasy, or some unfavorable flaw in his character. (Alternatively, Demas may have written down this epistle for Paul and is thus mentioned last and without praise.)

Demas fell away after having ministered with Paul, the great apostle! He saw his life and heard his teachings, and walked with Jesus for a while, yet fell away. Moreover, Paul didn't blame himself for Demas' own choice of apostasy.

### 4:15-17. VARIOUS GREETINGS TO FRIENDS.

**15 Give my greetings to the brothers at Laodicea, and to Nympha and the church in her house.**

***Nympha.*** Greek may be masculine or feminine.

---

[313] *To the church of God in Corinth… (1 Cor. 1:2)*

[314] *…Aquila and Priscilla greet you warmly in the Lord, and so does the church that meets at their house. (1 Cor. 16:19)*

[315] *The churches in the province of Asia send you greetings … (1 Cor. 16:19)*

[316] *for Demas, because he loved this world, has deserted me and has gone to Thessalonica. Crescens has gone to Galatia, and Titus to Dalmatia. (2 Tim. 4:10)*

***the church in her house.*** Cf. Philemon 2[317]; Rom. 16:5[318]; 1 Cor. 16:19[319]; Acts 12:12.[320] The church in the New Testament usually met in houses. It was a long time before they met in official "church buildings."

**16** *After this letter has been read to you, see that it is also read in the church of the Laodiceans and that you in turn read the letter from Laodicea.*

***the letter from Laodicea.*** Another circular letter. This indicates a unity between the churches in the same geographical region, so that this could happen.

**17** *Tell Archippus: "See to it that you complete the work you have received in the Lord."*

The church is entrusted with the duty of exhorting one of its leaders. There is no necessary reason to infer any negligence on his part. His ministry is important and should be zealously fulfilled.

Thus, the leaders should exhort the people and the people should exhort the leaders. Leaders need encouragement, and they need to let people encourage them. Sometimes it is hard for leaders to receive this encouragement, but they need it.

## 4:18. PAUL'S PERSONAL GREETING.

**18** *I, Paul, write this greeting in my own hand. Remember my chains. Grace be with you.*

---

[317] *to Apphia our sister, to Archippus our fellow soldier and to the church that meets in your home: (Philemon 2)*

[318] *Greet also the church that meets at their house. Greet my dear friend Epenetus, who was the first convert to Christ in the province of Asia. (Rom. 16:5)*

[319] *The churches in the province of Asia send you greetings. Aquila and Priscilla greet you warmly in the Lord, and so does the church that meets at their house. (1 Cor. 16:19)*

[320] *When this had dawned on him, he went to the house of Mary the mother of John, also called Mark, where many people had gathered and were praying. (Acts 12:12)*

***Remember my chains.*** Remember that the one who loves you and warns you of the errors is in chains for the gospel. (Paul's chains would have moved over the paper as he signed his name.) Therefore they should deeply regard his words.

***I, Paul, write this greeting in my own hand.*** Paul added his signature to the letter which was written by someone else at his dictation.

# Selected Bibliography

Alford, Henry. (1980). *Alford's Greek Testament: An Exegetical and Critical Commentary.* Grand Rapids, MI: Baker Book House.

Brenton, Lancelot, C. L. (Trans.). (1970). *The Septuagint Version of the Old Testament: Greek and English.* Grand Rapids, MI: Zondervan Publishing House.

Eadie, John. (1856/1977). *Commentary on the Epistle of Paul to the Colossians.* Minneapolis, MN: James and Klock Christian Publishing Co.

Gundry, Robert H. (1994). *A Survey of the New Testament.* Grand Rapids, MI: Zondervan Publishing House.

Henry, Matthew. (1991). *Matthew Henry's Commentary on the Whole Bible.* Hendrickson Publishers, Inc.

Kittel, Gerhard & Gerhard Friedrich. (1968). *Theological Dictionary of the New Testament.* Grand Rapids, MI: Wm. B Eerdmans Publishing Co.

Morrish, George. (1976). *A Concordance of the Septuagint.* Grand Rapids, MI: Zondervan Publishing House.

Nicoll, W. Robertson (ed.). (1980). *The Expositor's Greek Testament.* Grand Rapids, MI: Wm. B Eerdmans Publishing Co.

Tenney, Merrill, C. (1978). *New Testament Survey.* Leicester, England: Inter-Varsity Press.

Vincent, M. R. (n.d.). *Word Studies in the New Testament.* McLean, VA: MacDonald Publishing Company.

Wall, Robert W. (1993). *Colossians & Philemon.* Downers Grove, IL: InterVarsity Press.

Webber, Malcolm. (1992). *The Blood of God.* Goshen, IN: Pioneer Books.

**Strategic Press**
www.StrategicPress.org

Strategic Press is a division of Strategic Global Assistance, Inc.
www.sgai.org

513 S. Main St. Suite 2
Elkhart, IN 46516
U.S.A

+1-844-532-3371 (LEADER-1)

www.ingramcontent.com/pod-product-compliance
Lightning Source LLC
Chambersburg PA
CBHW071738090426
42738CB00011B/2522